The Complete Soccer Team Defensive Training Routine

90-Minute Professional Level Unit & Team Defending Routine

By Marcus DiBernardo

Table of Contents

Introduction

For years I have been training team defending using various methods. Every pre-season I would drill my team day after day on individual, unit and team defending. After pre-season was over, I always wanted a better way to consistently train and rehearse our defensive tactics throughout the entire season. I wanted a 90-minute training session that re-enforced our entire defensive game plan in order to keep it fresh in the player's minds. This past year I was fortunate enough observe a coach from Portugal who spoke about his "Tactical Periodization" plan over a 10-month season. He used a defensive routine that taught his team's defensive game model in a 90-minute routine. Once every 7-10 days the team would perform the defensive routine, usually with some type of variation switching a few exercises to keep the players mentally challenged. The defensive routine would also include some overlap into other games phases. It is essential to teach the different game phases and the connection between the phases. In this case it is "Defensive Organization" working into "Attacking Transition" – meaning when the defense is in their shape defending and they win the ball the next phase of play would be for them to attack – (defensive organization to attacking transition). This book covers a complete 90-minute defensive team training routine with fundamental information concerning defensive concepts from my book "The Science of Soccer Team Defending". The 90-minute training routine can be modified as needed. I have included numerous exercises that can be added into the routine so you can customize it to fit your team. I hope you enjoy the book and as always feel free to email me with questions or comments at coachdibernardo@gmail.com

Team Defending Principles & Strategies

Before coaching team defensive drills it is important to have a fundamental understanding of the principles and strategies of team defending. These principles and strategies should be taught and reinforced in team defending training sessions and drills. The coach's ability to communicate these principles effectively with the players is critical to playing effective team defense.

Key Principles:

Line of Confrontation: A defined line that is the reference point indicating where to start applying defensive pressure.

Line of Restraint: A line that is a reference point that indicates where the defending unit (the backline) would be pushed up to. The line of confrontation and line of restraint together help the team keep proper shape and compactness.

I use four basic lines of confrontation when teaching team defense. The line of restraint will naturally push up or back with the line of confrontation. The four lines of confrontation will be full, three quarters, half and one quarter. Choosing where to set the line of confrontation involves many factors. Things to consider are the speed of the other teams attacking players, the ability of the opponent to possess the ball, the fitness level of your team, the weather conditions, the score, up or down a man, the ability of your team to counter and the speed of oppositions back four.

Below are the diagrams of each of the lines of confrontation and restraint. The lines of confrontation are in red while the lines of restraint are in blue (#1 line of confrontation matches with #1 line of restraint and 2-4 as well).

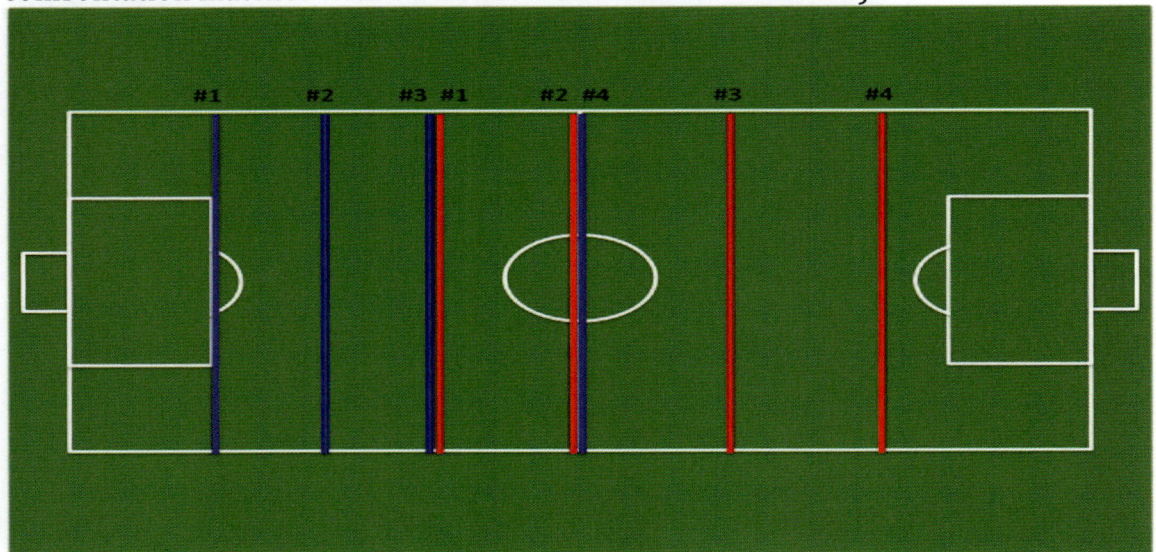

When holding a line of confrontation the coach can have players hold a very strict line or allow groups of 1-3 players to extend pressure over the line. There can be a number of reasons to extend pressure, especially if your team is using a high line of confrontation. If the opposition's back four is allowed to collect the ball comfortably right behind the line of confrontation they can easily serve penetrating balls over the top. I do not recommend letting teams feel comfortable on the ball and allowing them to hit unpressured long passes. I let my players extend pressure especially when the ball is being passed to a defender with his head down. At that point 1-3 players will break the line of confrontation and try to create turnover leading to a counter-attack.

Compactness: This is a basic principle in team defense. When a team is not in possession their objective is to make the field as small as possible for the attacking team. Creating a numerical advantage in the area of the ball is the goal of defensive compactness. The goal of the attacking team is to open the field up making the defense spread out. Spreading the field will open up gaps for the attacking team to penetrate through. In order to circulate the ball effectively, the team in possession must try and open up the field. The defensive team will be trying to do the exact opposite. When the ball is lost is this starts transition. Transition is one of the most important times in a soccer game. The team that was spread out will be trying to become compact and the team who was compact will be trying to spread out. That is a simple explanation but it is an important aspect of the game to understand. How a team manages transition from attacking to defending and defending to attacking can determine the outcome of the game.

In the illustration below the red team is showing good defensive compactness while sitting back in a low defensive block.

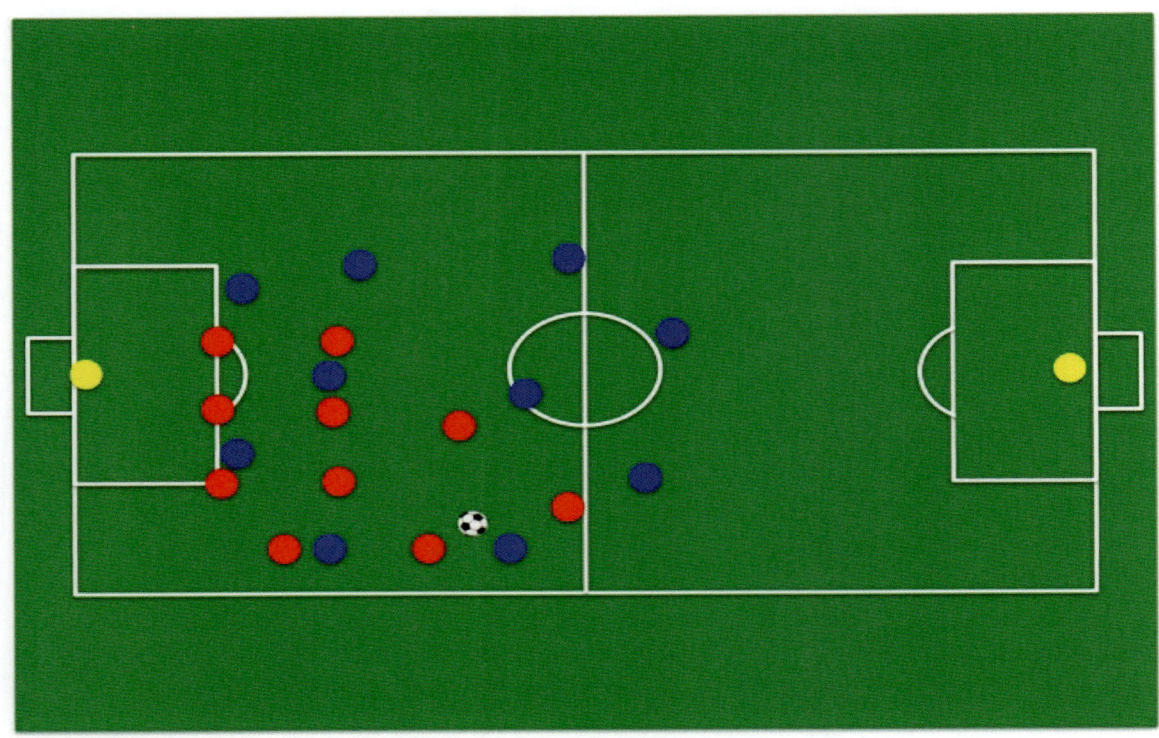

Pressing: When a team decides to press onto the opponent and force a turnover. This is a very aggressive tactic that requires players have a strong mental and fitness level to execute well. Pressing also requires the elimination of passing options and frequent double-teaming. Effective pressing requires intelligent positioning by players. Teams can press high up the field or employ aggressive zonal pressing based upon their line of confrontation. Pressing can also be looked at as a full press, half press, fake press and sitting back. The challenge of pressing comes when the opposition breaks the press.

The picture below shows four Blue players effectively pressing five Red players. Notice how #1&#2 for Blue leave their men to press while taking away passing angles. Ideally blue would have a numerical advantage but even numbers down with proper positioning blue can take away passing angles and press.

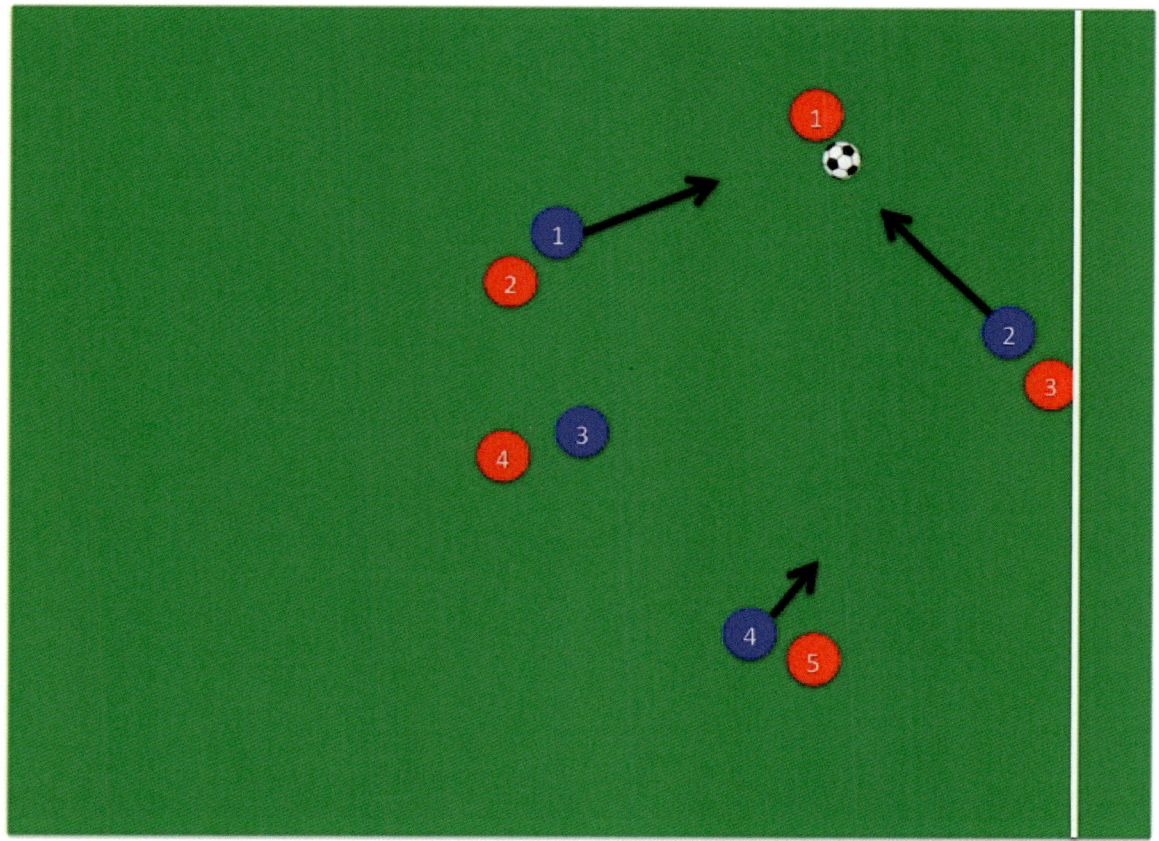

Full Press: Total commitment as a team pushing into the opponent and using a high line of confrontation while extending pressure.

Below is the team shape of a full press. The red line is the line of confrontation and the blue line the line of restraint.

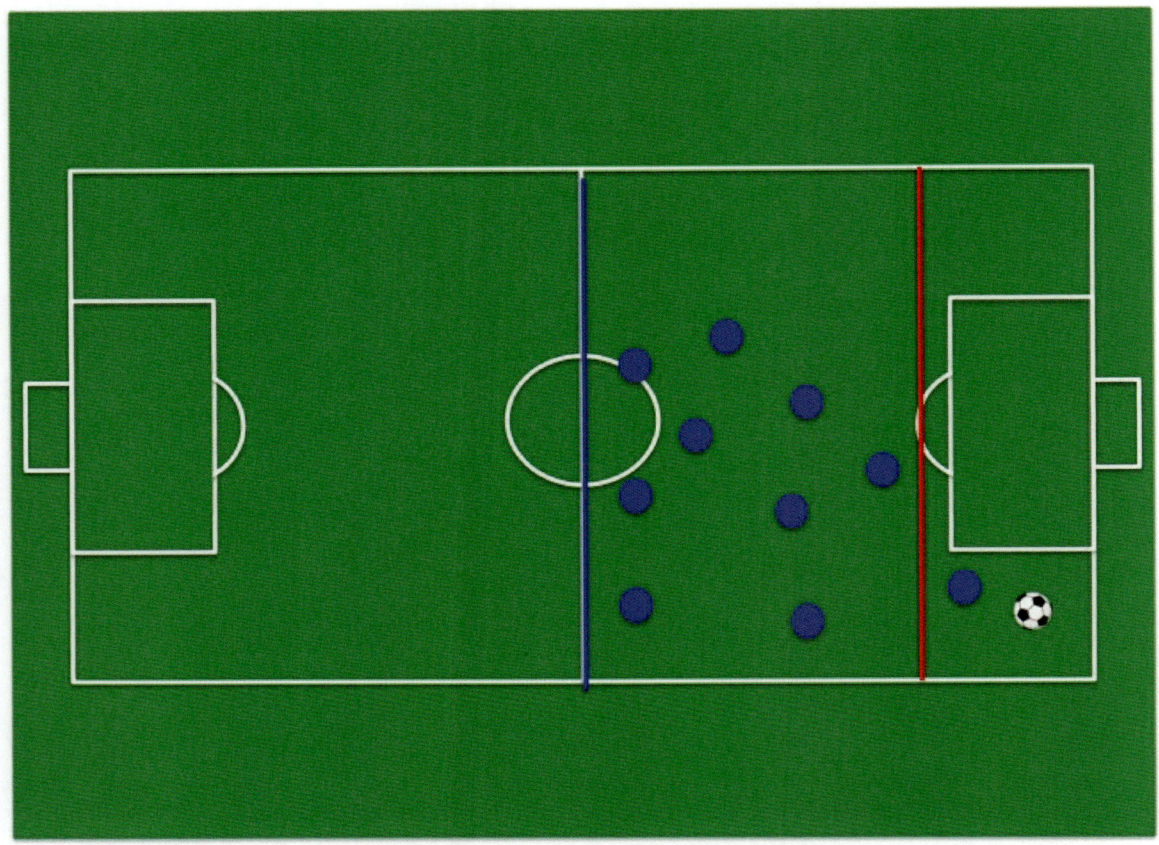

Half-Press: Setting the line of confrontation around half-field. Once the opponent comes close to the line of confrontation high pressure is applied in the zone.

Below is the team shape in the half-press. The red line is the line of confrontation and the blue line is the line of restraint.

Aggressive Zonal Pressing: I personally use aggressive zonal pressing with my team. The idea is to have the team drop off to a certain line of confrontation and force play into pre-determined designated areas where pairs of players will press the ball aggressively. The team understands that in those designated pressing areas we will try and start our counter attacks from. Aggressive zonal pressing is a variation of pressing that can be very effective if done correctly. Jose Mourinho has used aggressive zonal pressing to great success over his career with some of the largest clubs in the world.

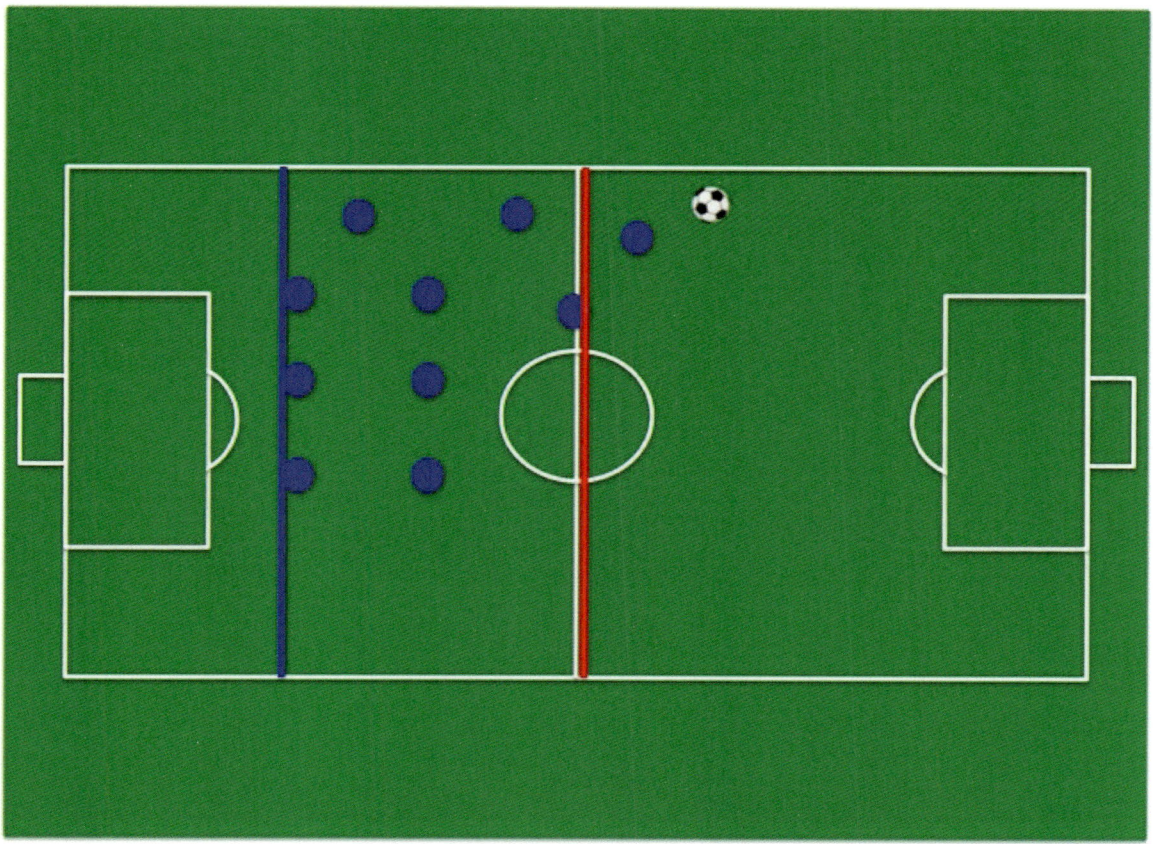

Sitting Back: The defensive team elects to set the line of confrontation inside their own half of the field. It is crucial to defend the dangerous area when sitting back. The dangerous area is the penalty box extended out 15 yards. That is the area most goals are scored from and assists are made. Wider areas and areas outside 30 yards from goal are less important to defend.

Below is a picture of a team with a low defensive block sitting back. The red line is the line of confrontation and the blue line is the line of restraint.

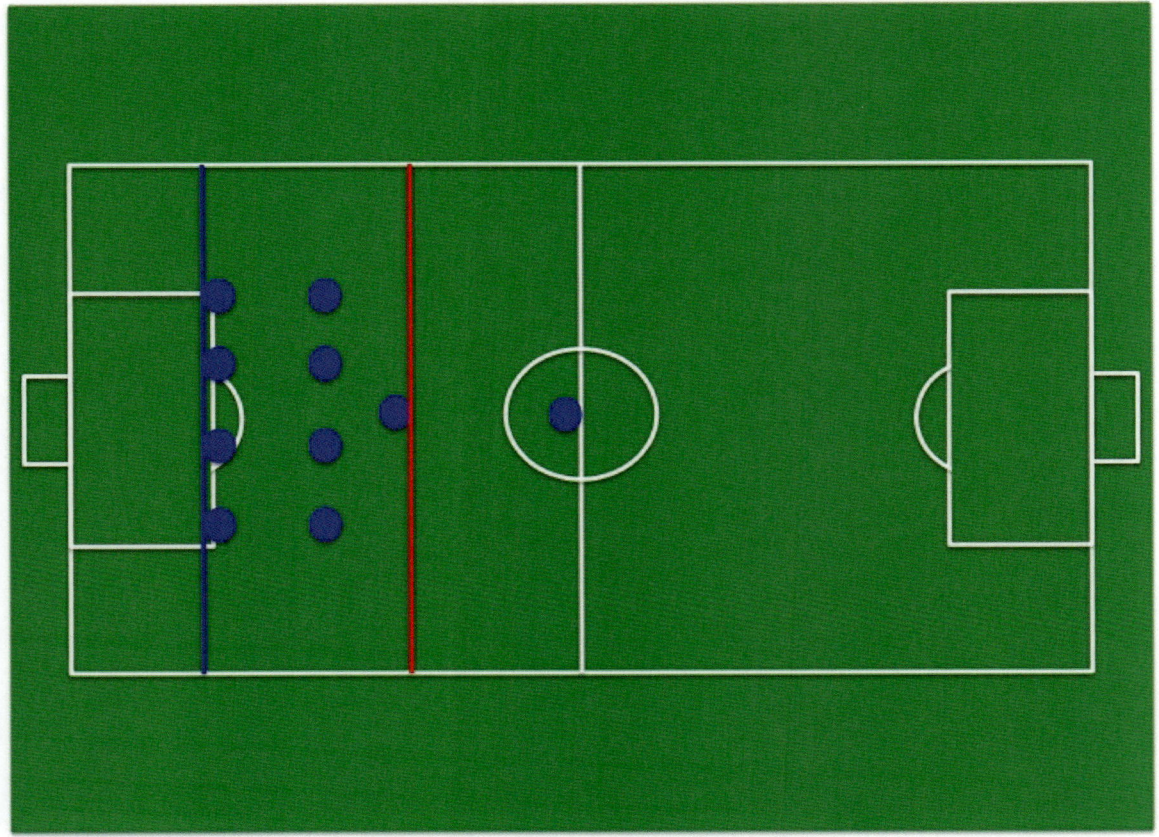

Fake Press: When a team gives the impression they are going to press but do not. They may elect to send 1-2 players to press on their own as the rest of the team sits or even drops back a little.

Zonal Defending: Each player in theory covers a zone on the field. When an opponent comes into the defenders zone he will mark that player. As the attacker leaves the zone the defender will pass the attacker onto another defender in the next zone. When passing attacker on to the next defender there should be visual and verbal communication.

The below picture shows zonal defending and the passing on of players. F2 on red will be passed on from the right center back to the left center back as F2 enters into the next zone. M2 on red is making a run between the midfield and back lines of the blue team. This will cause a problem for the blue team. When a midfielder runs between the lines they must be tracked and marked. The solution is for a back line player to step up and mark the midfielder (this may cause the back line to lose shape) or the midfielder player to track back (causing a problem in transition when the ball is won and leaving open space in the midfield). Zonal defending is about problem solving and proper positioning to minimize passing and shooting options.

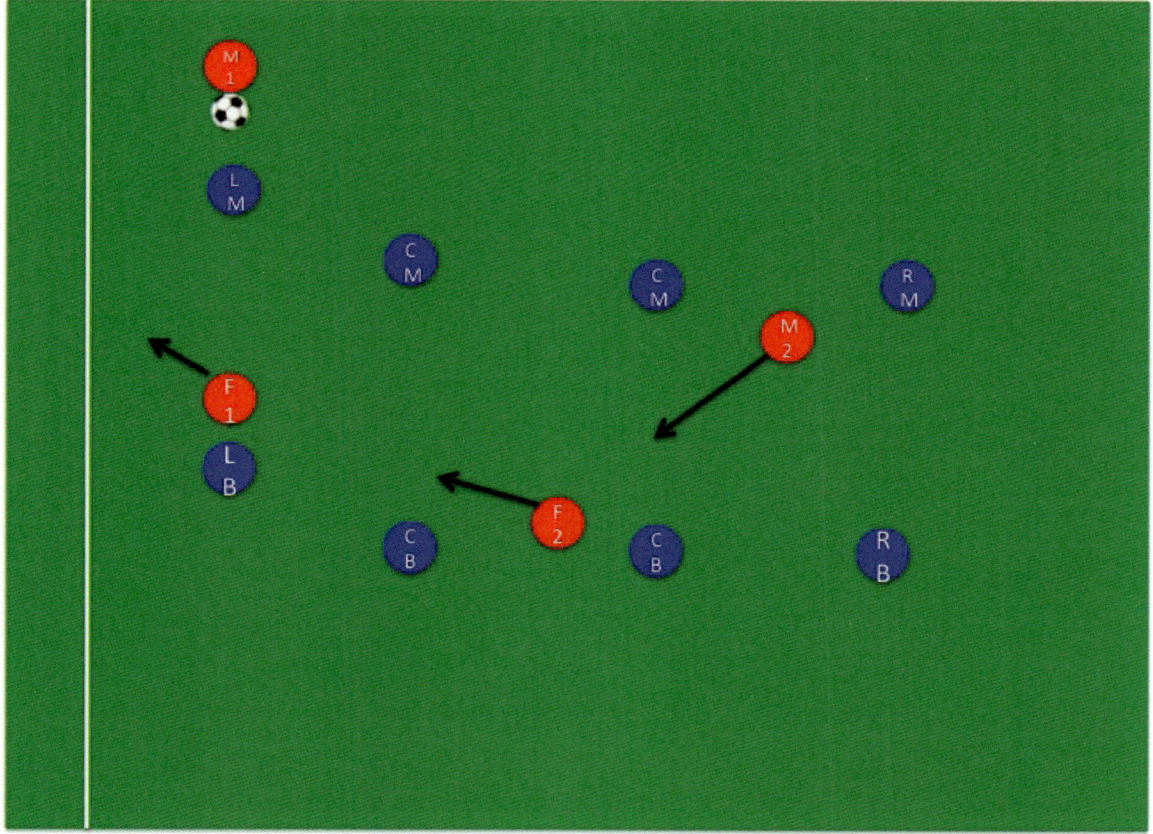

Defensive Shifting: When a player shifts over to make sure all the attackers are covered. Example: If the right back has two players to cover the right center back can shift onto the unmarked attacker. If the right center back was marking a player before the shift the left center back would take the right center backs player allowing him to shift.

Shifting is a way of problem solving. Being able to problem solve is very important when defending. The attacking team wants to use movement, positioning and overloads to unbalance and confuse the defense. The defenders must work together to solve the problems of the attacker's movements, which why attacker like to play in between the defense and midfield lines. Meaning a striker that checks into the midfield can trouble a defender. Should the defender get pulled out of position and follow the attacker? Does the attacker by checking into the midfield create an attacking overload at midfield? Do the defending midfielders run with the attacking midfielders into the defensive back line? Problem solving is a very important skill to teach your team.

The below picture shows the back-line performing a defensive shift. The left back has two players and needs help. In this case the left center back can shift over and pick up the extra player.

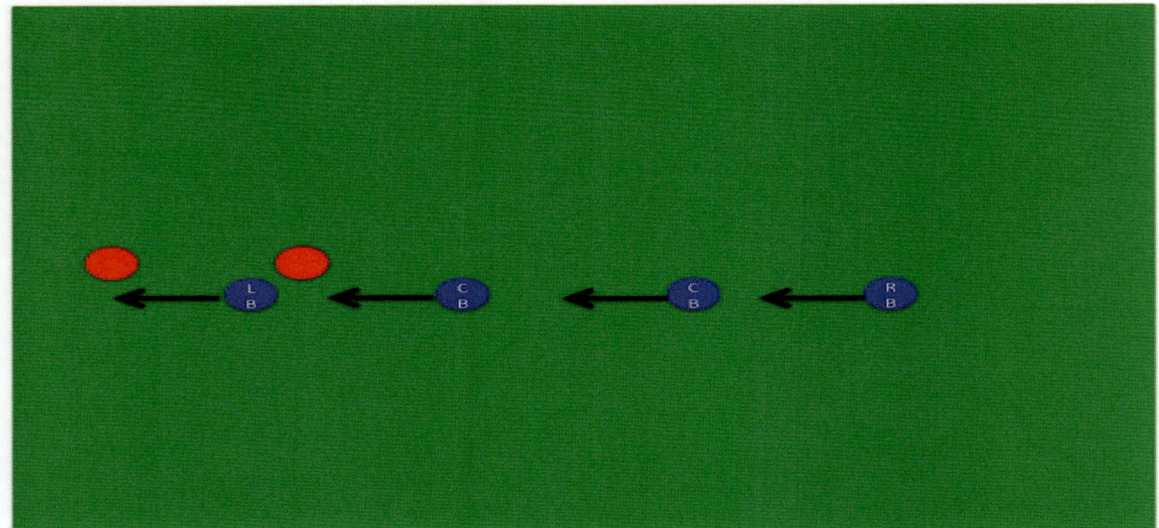

Pressure, Cover and Balance: 1st Defender, 2nd Defender, 3rd Defender. Understanding the roles of the 1st, 2nd and 3rd defenders is critical. The first defender will dictate the positions taken up by the second and third defenders. The job of the first defender is to slow play down and try to make play predictable. The job of the second defender is to support the first defender in case he is beaten and eliminate forward passing. The third defender gives the team balance and takes away further passing angles. These are the general responsibilities of the defenders. The game moves fast so reacting quickly to solve problems is essential.

The below picture demonstrates the basic principle of pressure, cover and balance and the lines of cover. The left back is the pressure, the left center back is the cover (45 degree angle back), the right center back is the balance and the right back is the balance as well. In dotted white line shows the lines of defensive depth. In the first example there are two lines of depth. In the second example there are three lines of defensive depth. Three lines of depth is safer but it also makes holding the offside's trap more difficult.

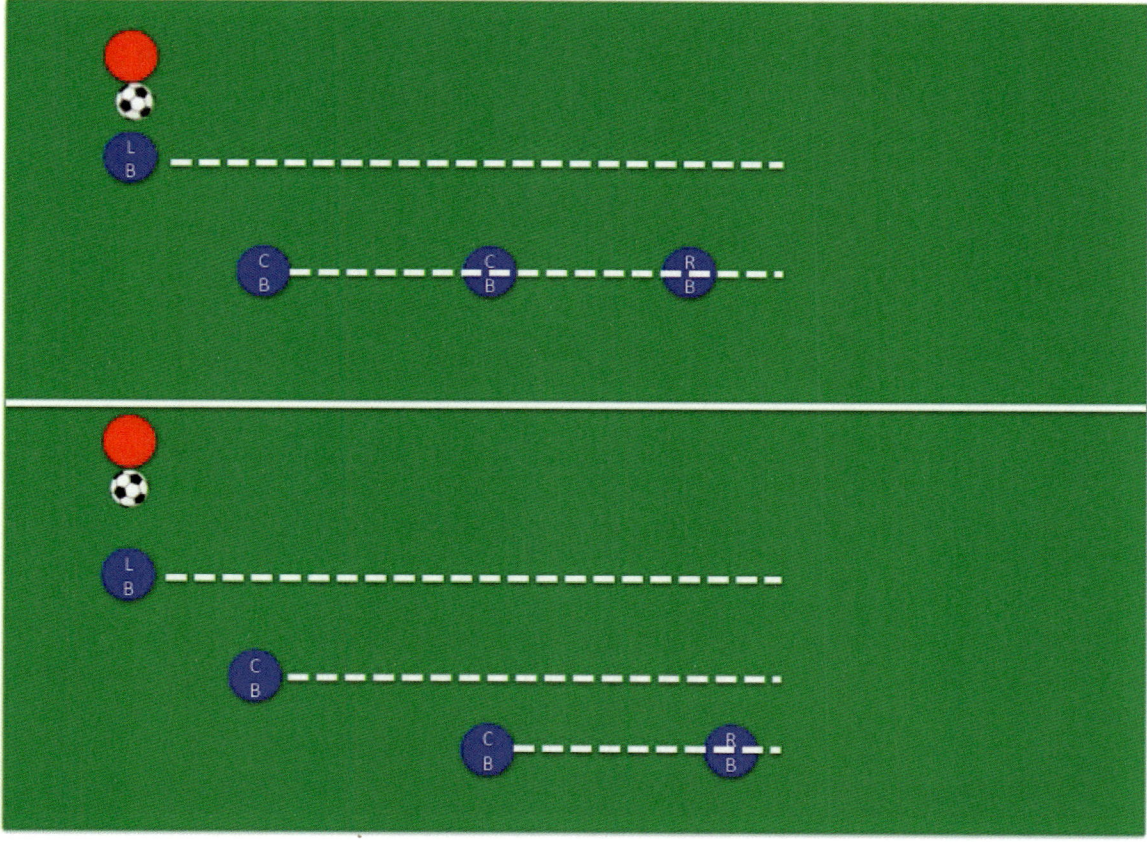

Key Words that Provide the Defensive Team Directions:

Slide Right: The team should collectively move to the right in order to achieve compactness. The team will be following the direction of the ball.

Slide Left: The team should collectively move to the left in order to achieve compactness. The team will be following the direction of the ball.

Hold: The team does not advance up the field. Especially the back line and midfield. It is possible the forward and another player can go one their own and press when the rest of the team is holding.

Drop: The entire team drops back. This is done when there is no pressure on the ball and the attacking team has a chance to go forward quickly. The defense needs to buy time to get organized and cut-off the dangerous space behind the defensive line. When there is no pressure on the ball and the team stretches backwards it can be called becoming "elastic".

Step: This is when the entire team pushes up the field. This happens when the attacking team plays the ball backwards and can't play forward right away or the player on the ball is forced to dribble backwards. By pushing on it squeezes the attacking team into a compact space.

Show-in: Tells the first defender to push the attacker with the ball inside.

Show-out: Tells the first defender to push the attacker with the ball outside towards the sideline.

Back Left: The second defender lets the first defender know he has cover behind to the left.

Back Right: The second defender lets the first defender know he has cover behind to the right.

Double: When a teammate is pressing the player with the ball and wants you to help press as well. This creates a situation with two defenders against one attacker.

Goal Side: The defender positions himself between the player he is marking and the goal. You might here coaches or players yell out "get goal side".

Zones of Responsibility by Position

This full field grid is designed to provide the general responsibilities for players in the back and midfield units. The visual zones help players stay disciplined in their defensive shape. I mark the grid out with cones on the field. The LB & LM cover Zone#1 & 2. The LCB & LCM cover Zones #1,2 & 3. The RCB & RCM cover Zones #2,3 & 4. The RB & RM cover Zones #4 & 3.

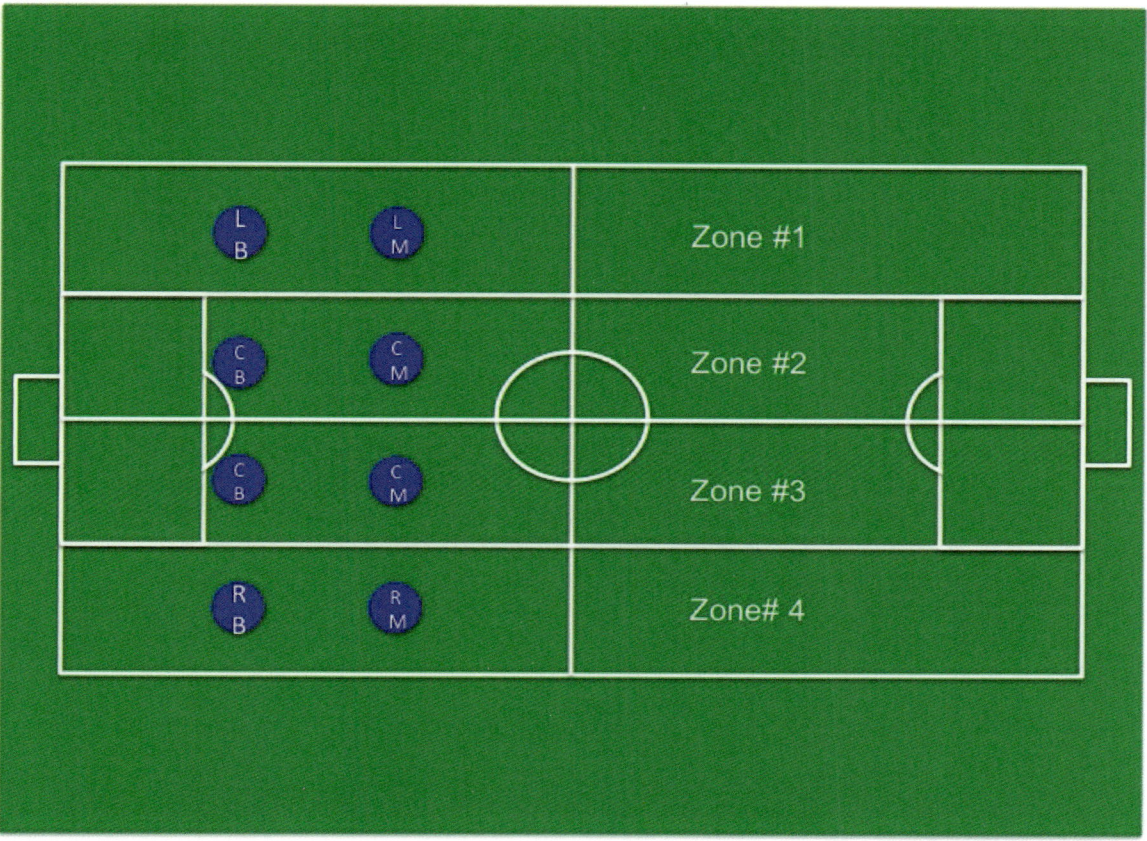

When training your team it is important to apply the principles of team defense that I just covered. The drills are there to create the environment but the coach must guide and teach the team using sound defensive principles.

90-Minute Team Defensive Routine

The 90 minute defensive routine is designed to flow from one exercise to the next, moving from simple to complex and unit to team. It can be adjusted to fit larger numbers of players as well. Pick the exercises that you prefer and feel free to customize the routine. I provide you with enough exercises to have options when it comes to varying the routine. Keep the tempo, intensity and concentration levels high. It is important to train this routine at a game realistic speed and intensity level. I recommend varying the routine slightly every week in order to keep the training new and challenging for the players. Your specific routine should directly be in line with your game model. Training Model = Game Model. This is a basic principle in all "Tactical Periodization Training". If you need information on Tactical Periodization I have a book called "Tactical Periodization: Made Simple" that explains the training method in detail. Enjoy the training routine and I am confident your team will benefit from the training.

Exercise #1)
The coach will call out a color and number. The players will have to react quickly and take the appropriate defensive shape according to the number & color. I have shown the example in three different positions with the coach calling out Red 1 first, then Red 2 and last Red 3. I gave these examples to show the correct pressure cover and balance positions for the unit defenders. The coach would normally call out different colors and numbers making the players shift from white to red to blue etc.
Coach Calls Red #1 – this is would be the correct defensive shape

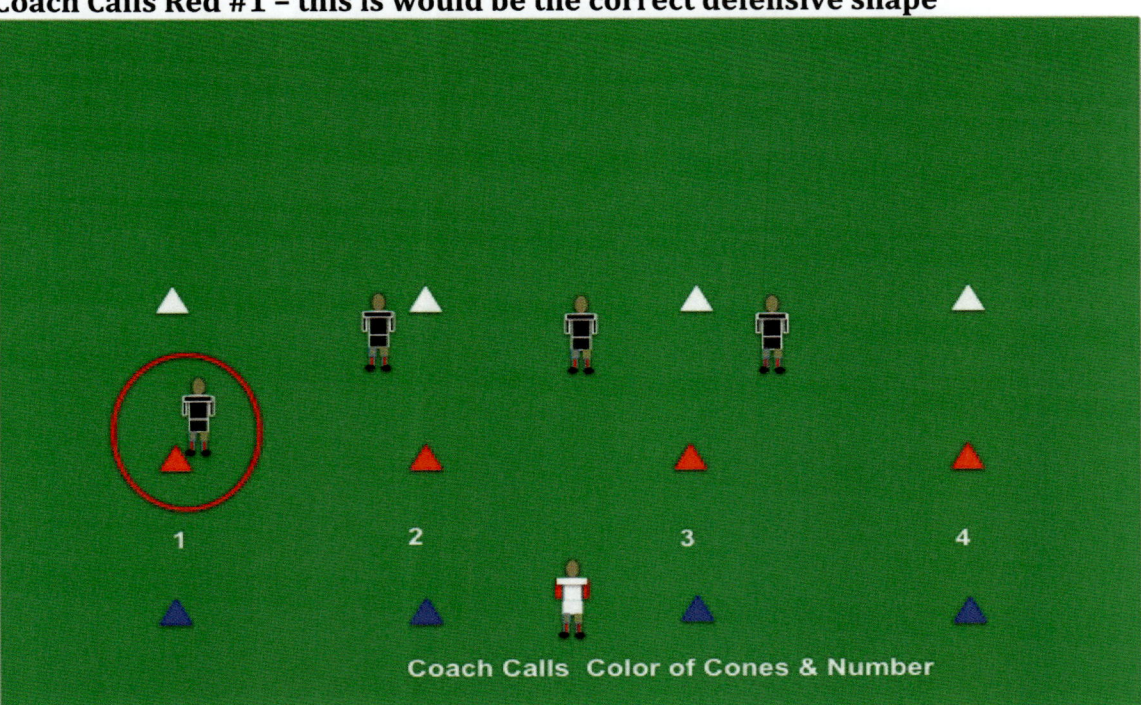

Coach Calls Color of Cones & Number

Coach Calls Red #2 – this would be correct defensive shape

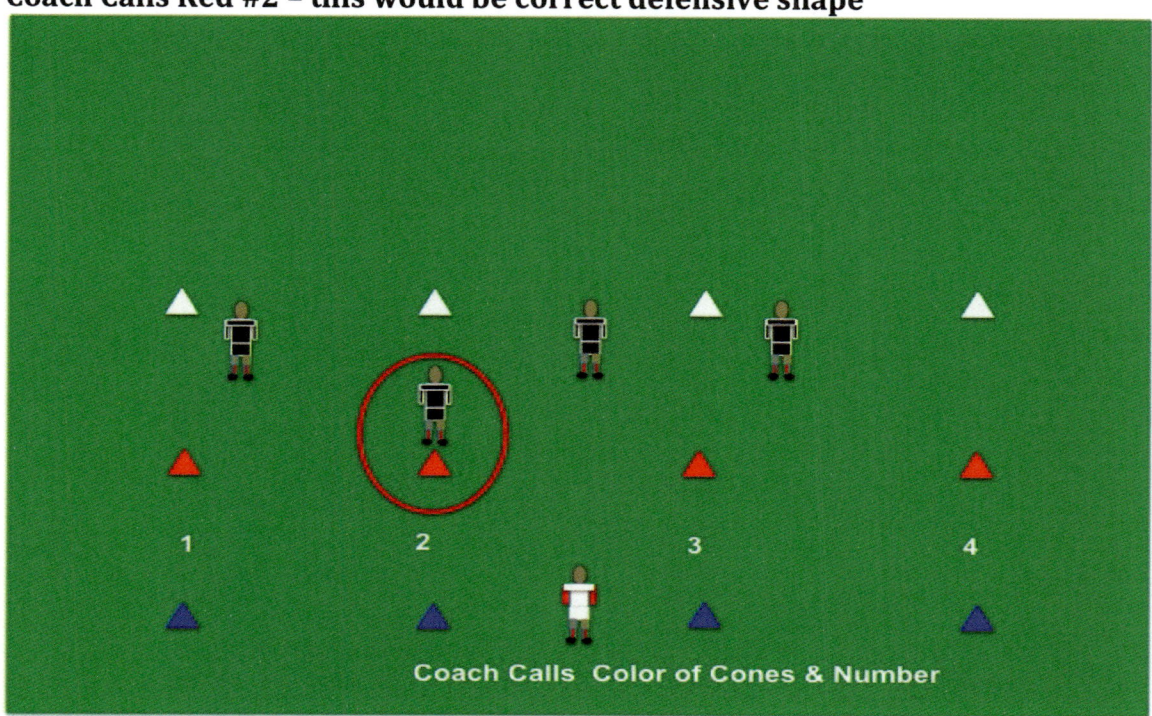

Coach Calls Red #3 – this is correct defensive shape

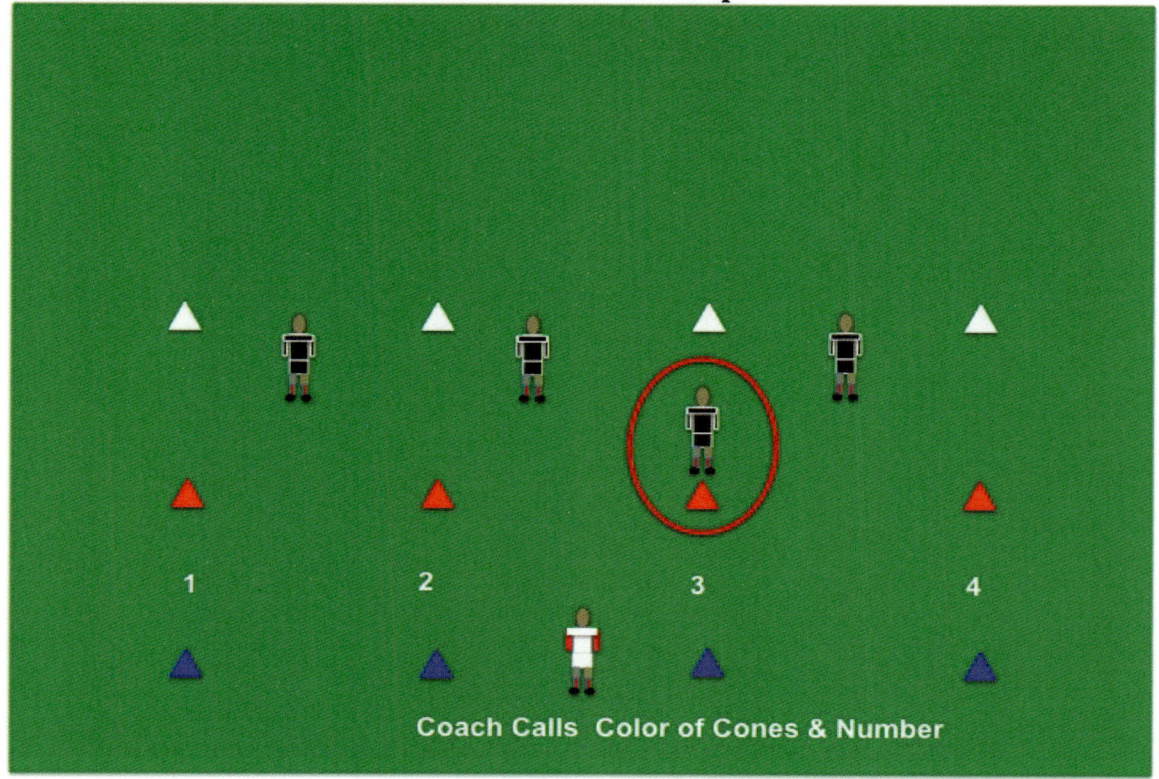

Exercise #2)

The defensive unit shown in blue works on proper positioning using pressure, cover and balance while forming triangles (shown in red). The black team moves the ball as they look to hit a penetrating pass to the red players on the other side. All play is 2-touch. Only one pressuring blue player can extend pressure into the opposing teams grid. If the penetrating pass is successful, the red team of two players will pass back and forth until they can hit a penetrating ball into the black team. The blue team is constantly working on proper shape and positioning.

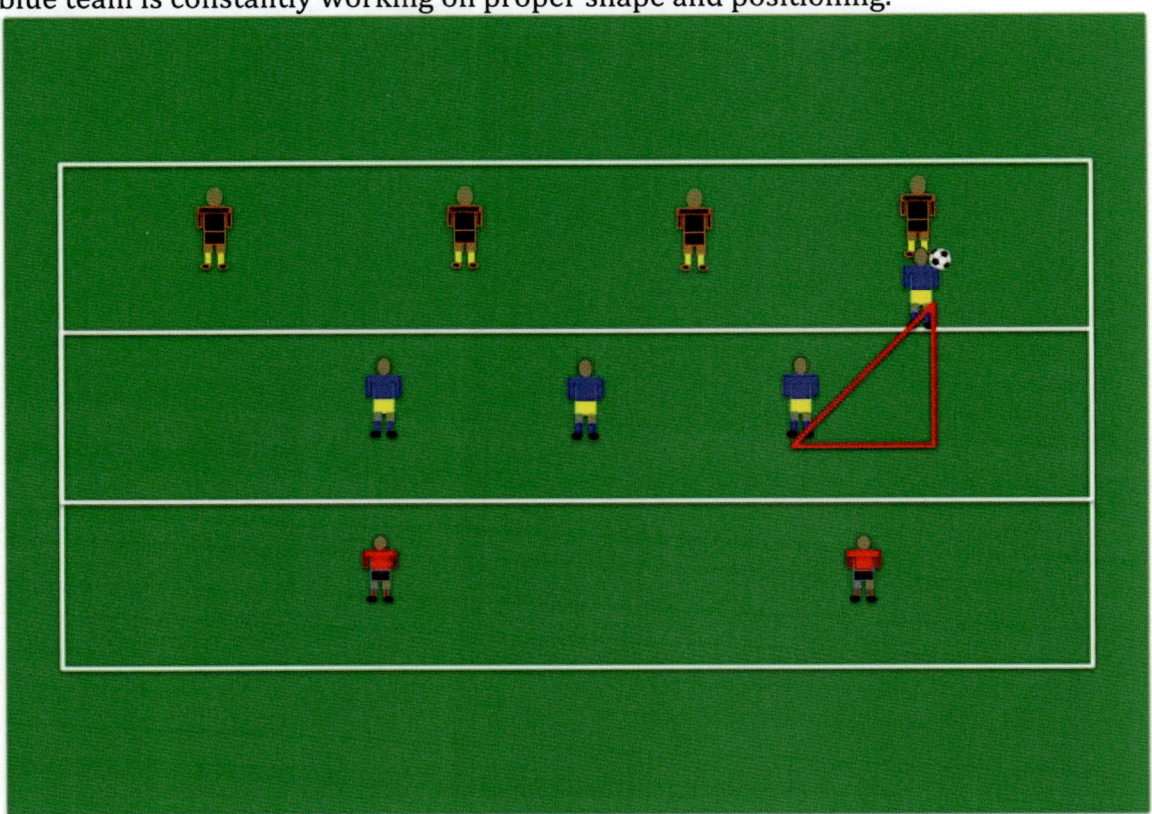

Modified for Midfield Unit:
The only difference in this example is that we are looking at the midfield unit instead of the back four defensive unit. Notice how the left center midfielder is dropped extra deep – creating a third line of depth. The idea is to have a player in-between the defensive line and the midfield line. The space between the lines is where attackers like to operate. By dropping a midfield player in that gap it will help prevent the attacking team from exposing space and playing between the lines.

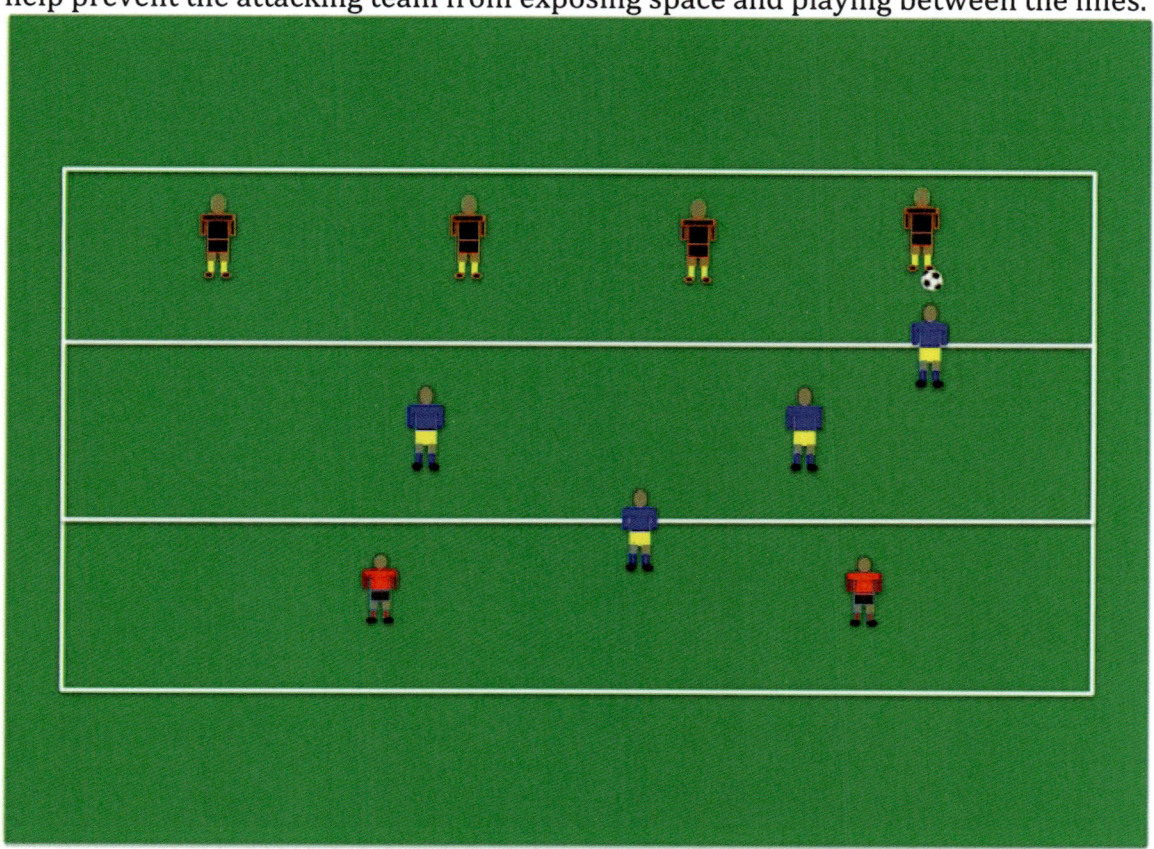

Exercise#3)
The red group represents the defensive unit. As the coach plays the ball into any random black player, the red defender must press-up onto the black player receiving the ball. The black player plays the ball back to the coach who plays it into a new black player who runs to receive the pass. The passes should be 1-touch in order to develop a quick rhythm to the exercise. The goal is not to intercept the pass, rather to get a rhythm of tracking players up and back from the defensive line.

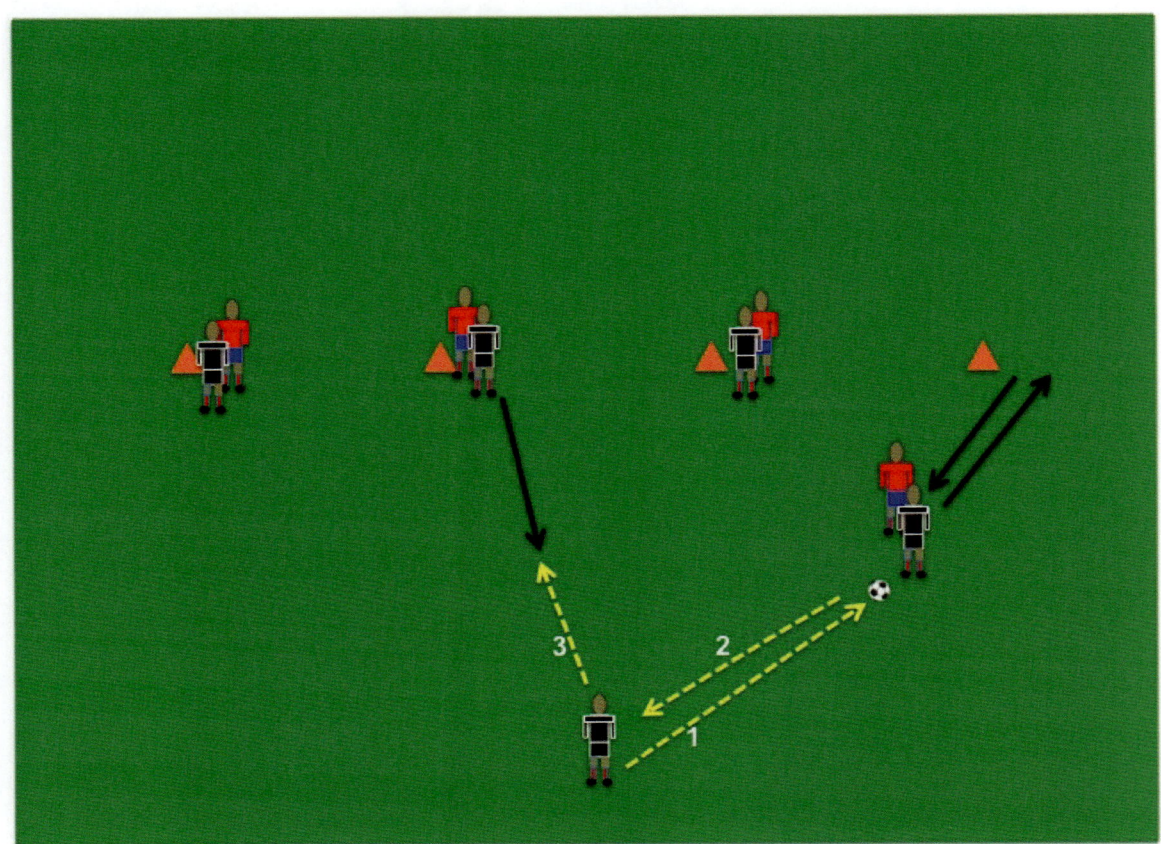

Exercise #4)
The blue team of four players rotates the ball as the black defensive unit must adjust to the ball position. Start by having the blue team stop the ball for 2 seconds after each pass to allow the black team to get in proper positions. After the black team improves and gets faster, the blue team can move the ball faster without stopping it.

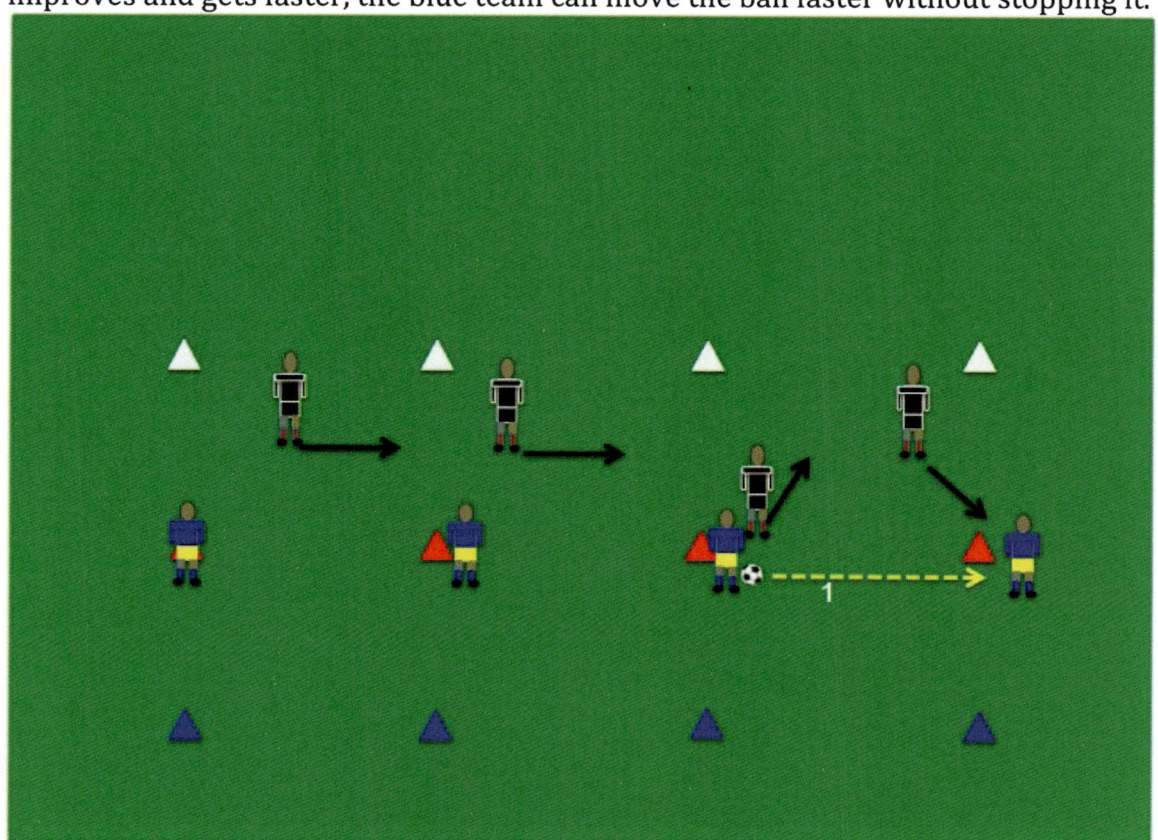

Exercise #5)
The coach dribbles across the defensive line as the players step to the coach and pressure him when he is in their zone. The entire line is always working and adjusting their positions together as a unit in relation to the coach dribbling across.

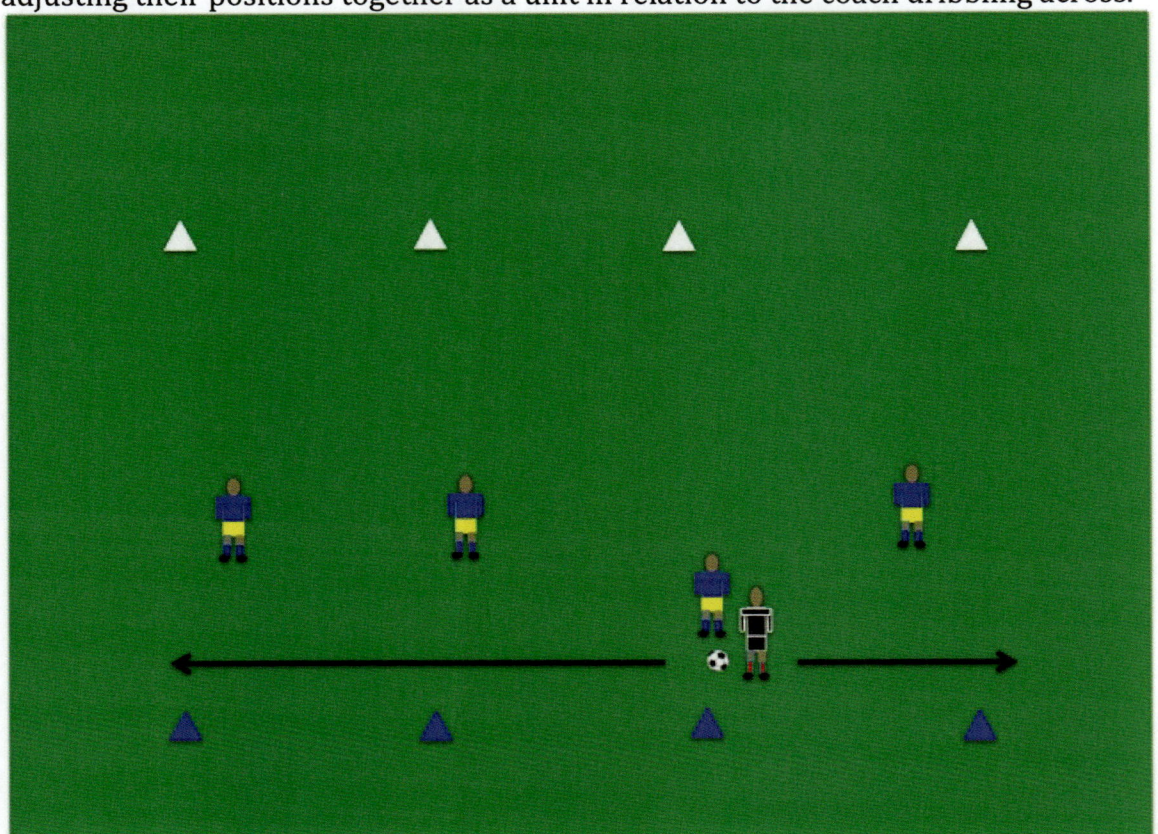

Exercise #6)
Now the coach will dribble horizontal and vertically at the defensive unit. The unit must adjust accordingly. The unit can retreat back to the white cones if the coach dribbles at them but they must hold their ground at the white cones. As the coach retreats back towards the blue cones the defensive line will push forward and make the space. As the coach dribble across, players will step to the ball.

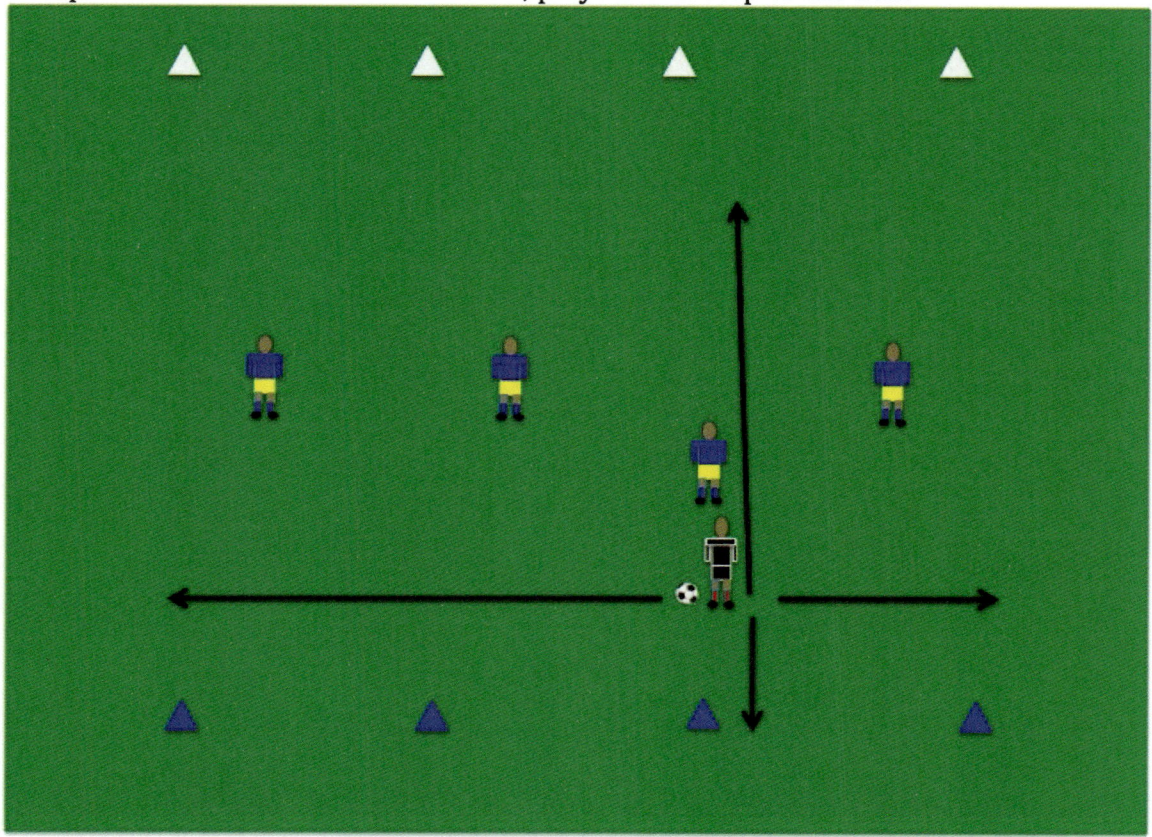

Exercise #7)

This is similar to exercise #6 but now we have added a goalkeeper and are training in the defensive 1/3 of the field. The back four defensive unit will adjust to the coach dribbling at them and across the field. If the coach dribbles straight at them the defensive unit will back up only to the edge of the 18 yard line. At that point they will need to hold the line and one player will leave the unit to confront the dribbler 1v1. As the dribbler retreats back the entire defense will press up.

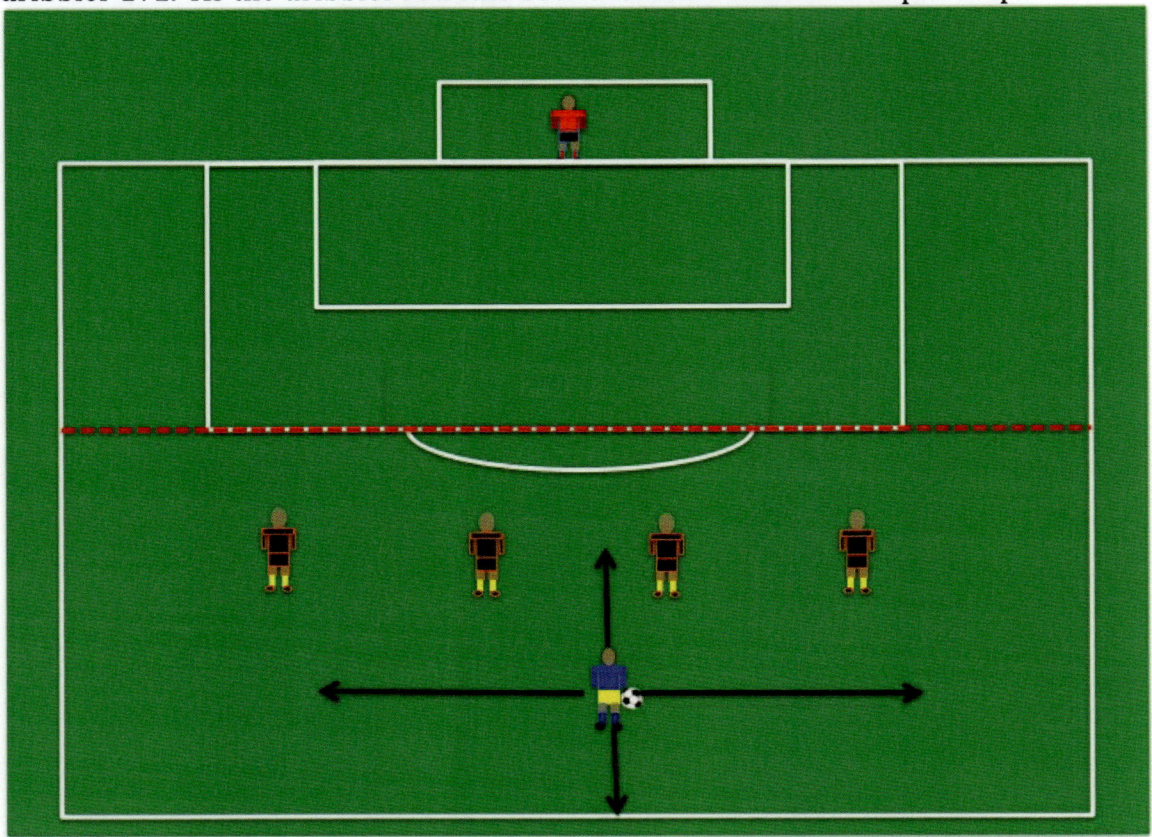

Exercise #8)
The coach will pass the ball to any of the cones as the player in back of the cone must sprint up and 1-touch the ball back to the coach. This exercise should keep a quick rhythm to it. It trains players to step up out of the line in their zone to pressure.

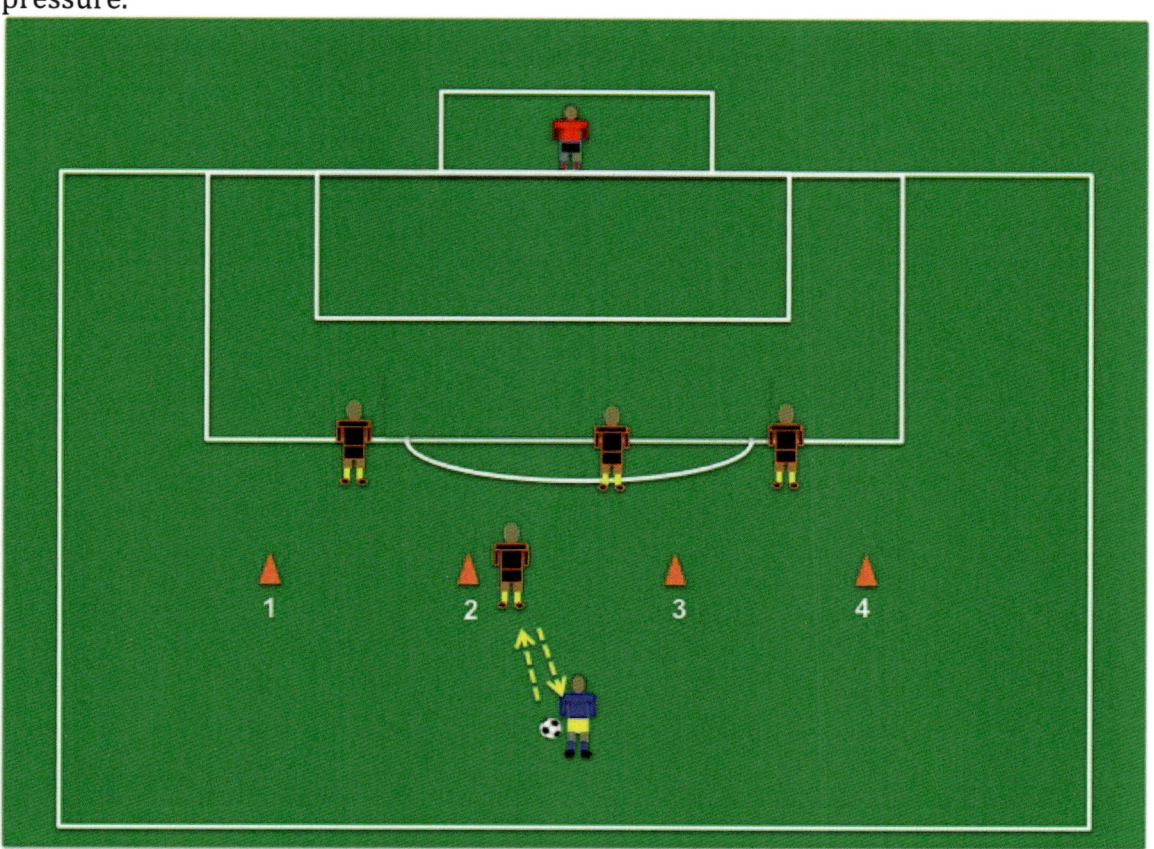

Exercise #9)
This exercise now challenges the player's as they must adjust to numerous different defending locations. Proper positioning of the back four is required for every location called. The "Red R" & "Red L" locations are the only locations where the back line will be flat across with no defensive depth or coverage. The purple and orange markers force the defensive unit to cover and defend wider areas. The yellow and blue cones are similar to the previous exercise's defending positions. The keeper can help direct all movements to ensure proper shape is used.

Exercise #10)

This exercise is 5v4. The objective is for the 5 offensive players to circulate the ball and make the back four unit adjust. Only when the ball is played into the lone forward in the middle a center back step up to cover him. If the center back steps up on the forward when the ball is out wide the back line will be exposed. The center back should only step when the ball is played into the forward.

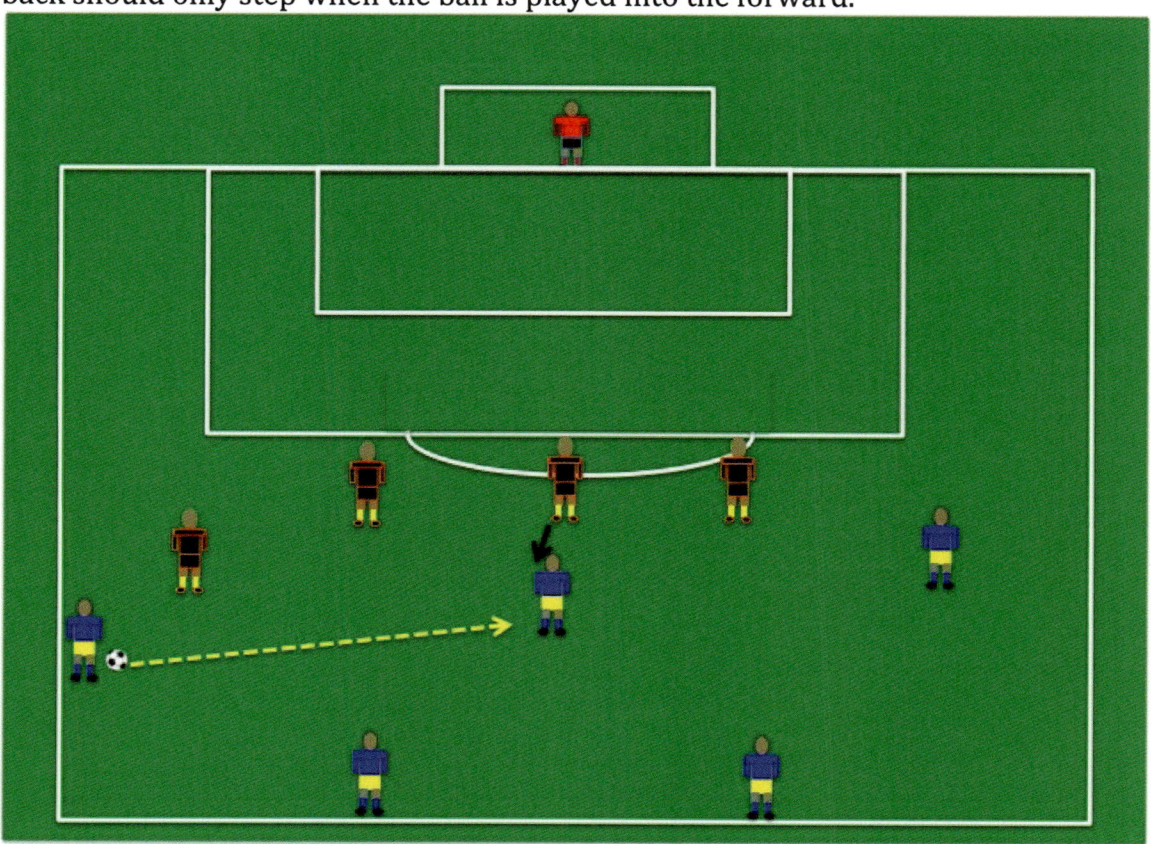

Exercise #11)

Now we progress to a 6v4. The ball will be circulated into all the blue players as the black/orange team adjusts. This exercise can be done without scoring – just to make the defense adjust. The progression would be to add scoring and make play live. Going from defensive organization to attacking transition. For now in the routine I would leave it without scoring.

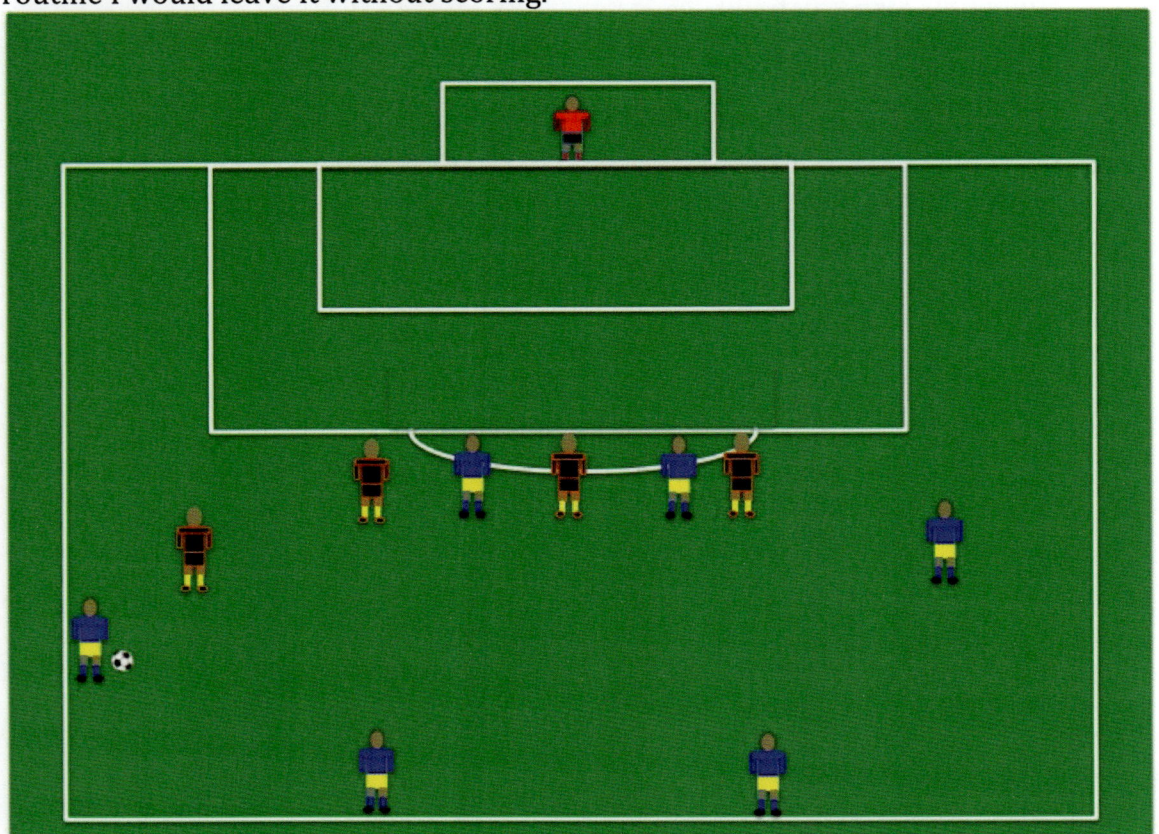

Exercise #12)

The next progression is 8v6 adding 2 center midfielders to the defending team. The 2 center midfielders serve to operate as a screen for balls being played into the forwards in front of the back four. If the ball is intercepted – the black team has 6 or less passes to score on the small-sided goals located at half field (2-touch limit). This exercise now goes from defensive organization to attacking transition.

Exercise #13)
The entire midfield "4" is now added to make two units of four players defending. Notice the shape of the midfield line with the LCM dropping into the space between the back 4 and midfield. This is a coaching preference. Whatever shape you wish your team to take is your choice. I would just make sure it fits logically into your game model. In this 4v8 exercise – the objective is only for the blue team to move the ball from side to side as the orange/black team work on adjusting their positioning in relation to the ball.

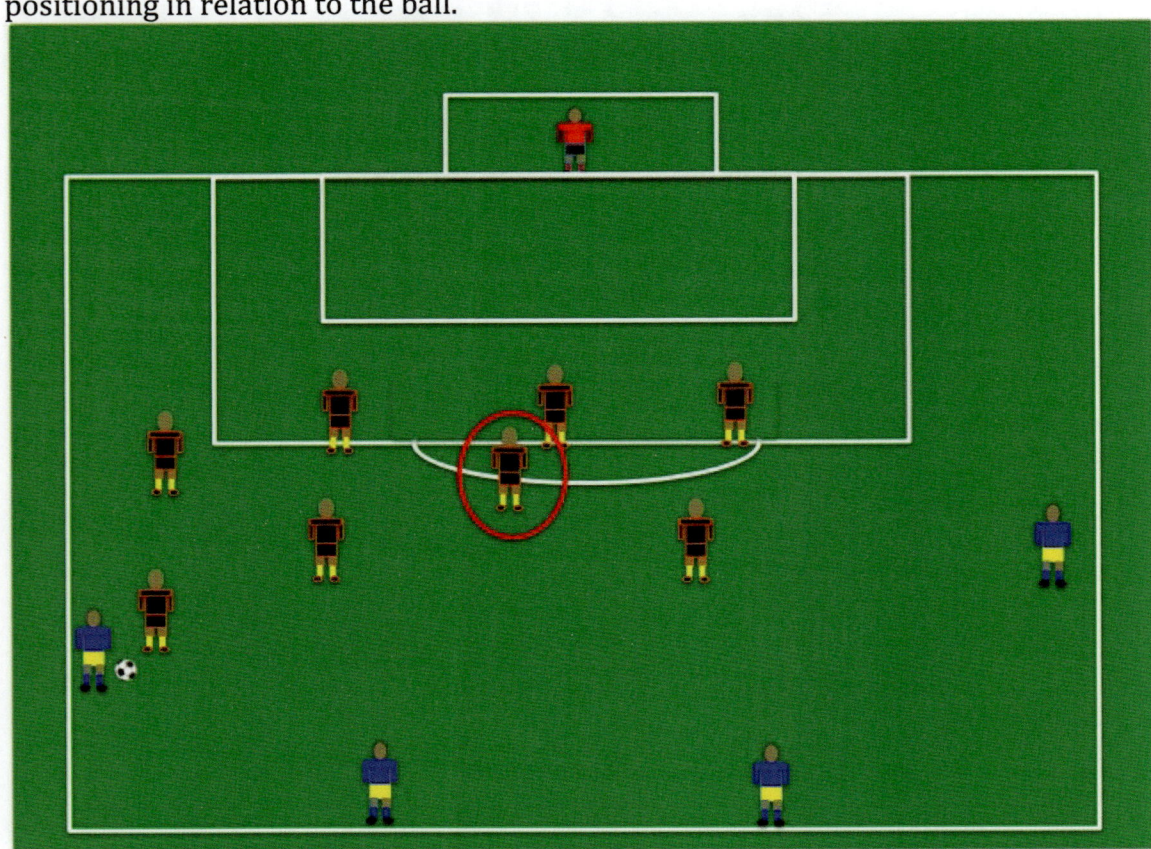

Exercise #15)
Building on the last exercise there are now 9 field players and a keeper for the orange/black team. The only player that is missing is the forward (playing a 4-2-3-1 system). The blue team is moves the ball and tries to circulate it from side to side and out wide. The orange/black team is looking to press the ball in the pre-determined pressing zones that are out lined in yellow. This exercise is meant to keep the orange/black team moving and adjusting, while working on aggressive zonal pressing inside the yellow boxes. You can eventually make this game live with counter goals similar to exercise #12.

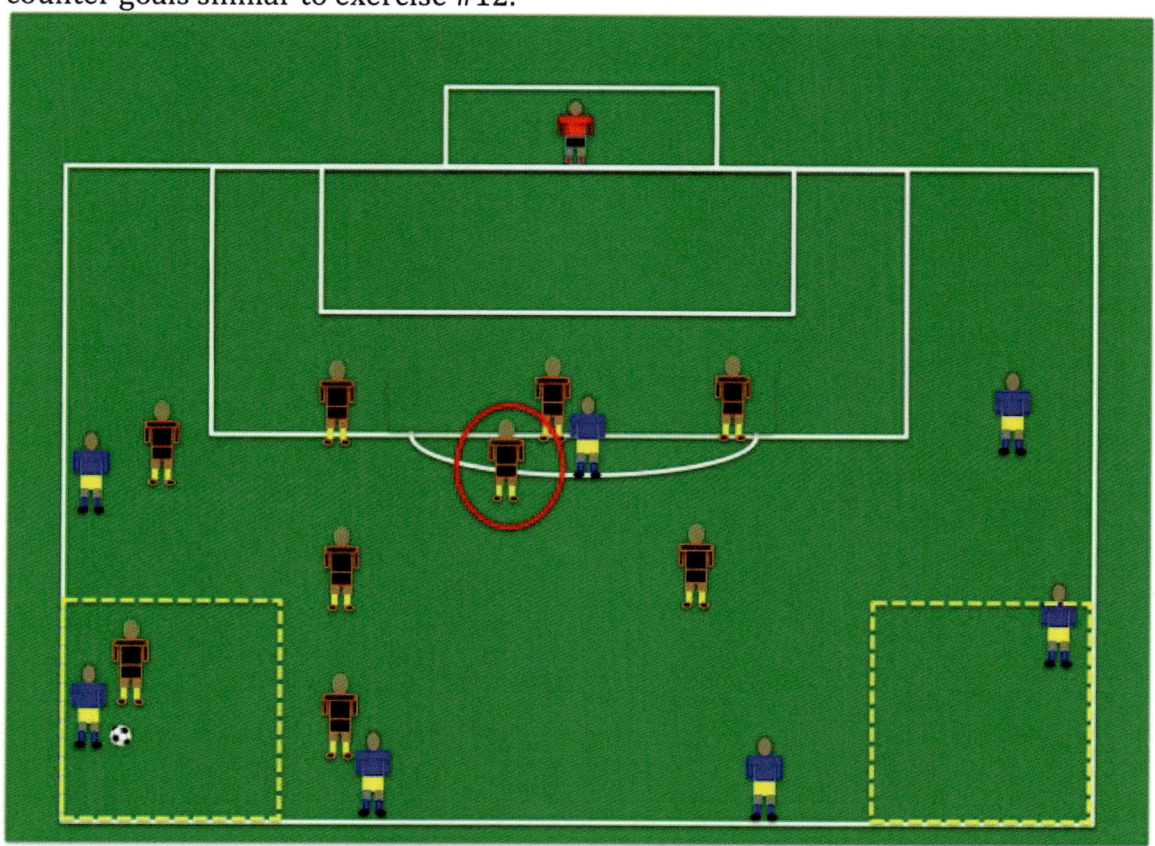

Exercise#16)

In this final exercise the goals are moved up to the top of 18-yard box and two lines of confrontation are marked-out. The blue team can't extend pressure with more than one player over the blue line when defending and the black/orange team can't extend pressure with more than one player over the black line when defending. Build the complexity by using the entire field and marking out the zones in which the defensive team will pressure and try to create turnovers.

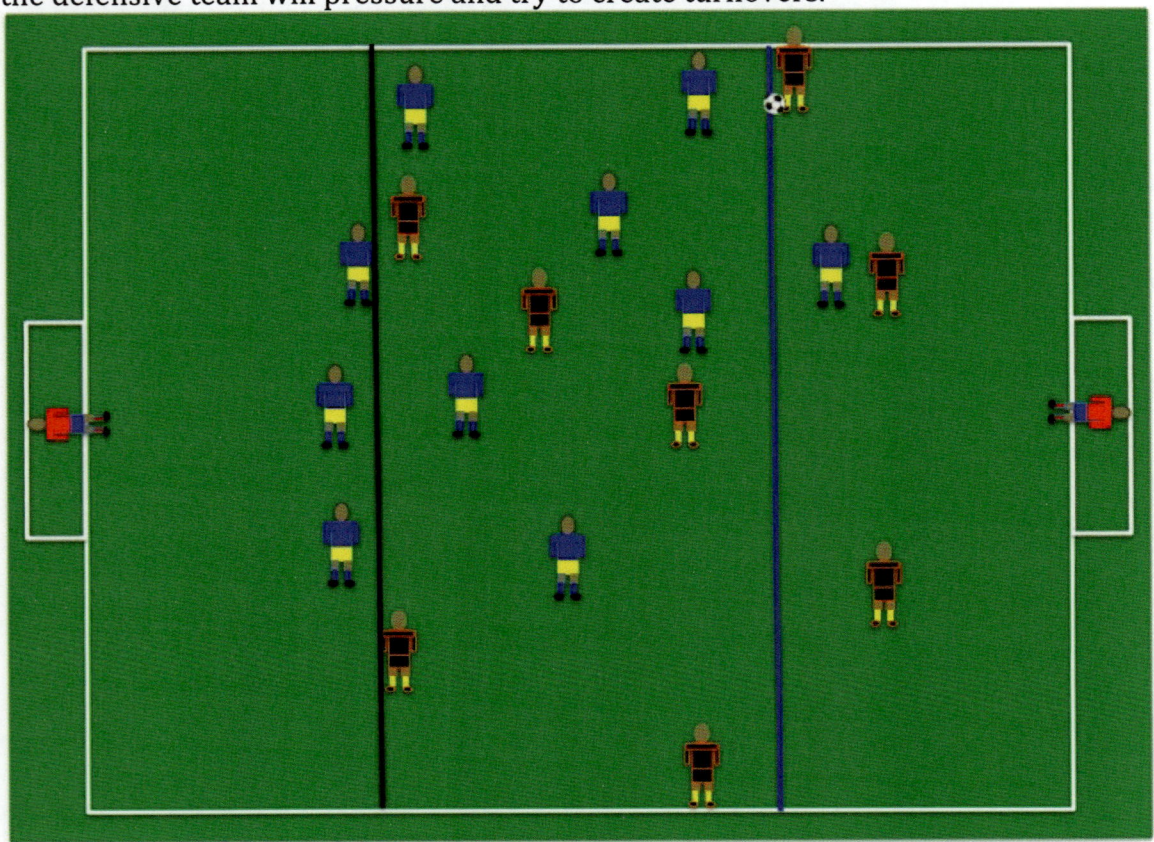

Additional Exercises That Can Be Added Into The Routine

Exercise #1)
The black/orange team will adjust positions as the blue team tries to work the ball from one target man on the outside to the other. One player at a time on the black/orange team can extend pressure into the blue's box.

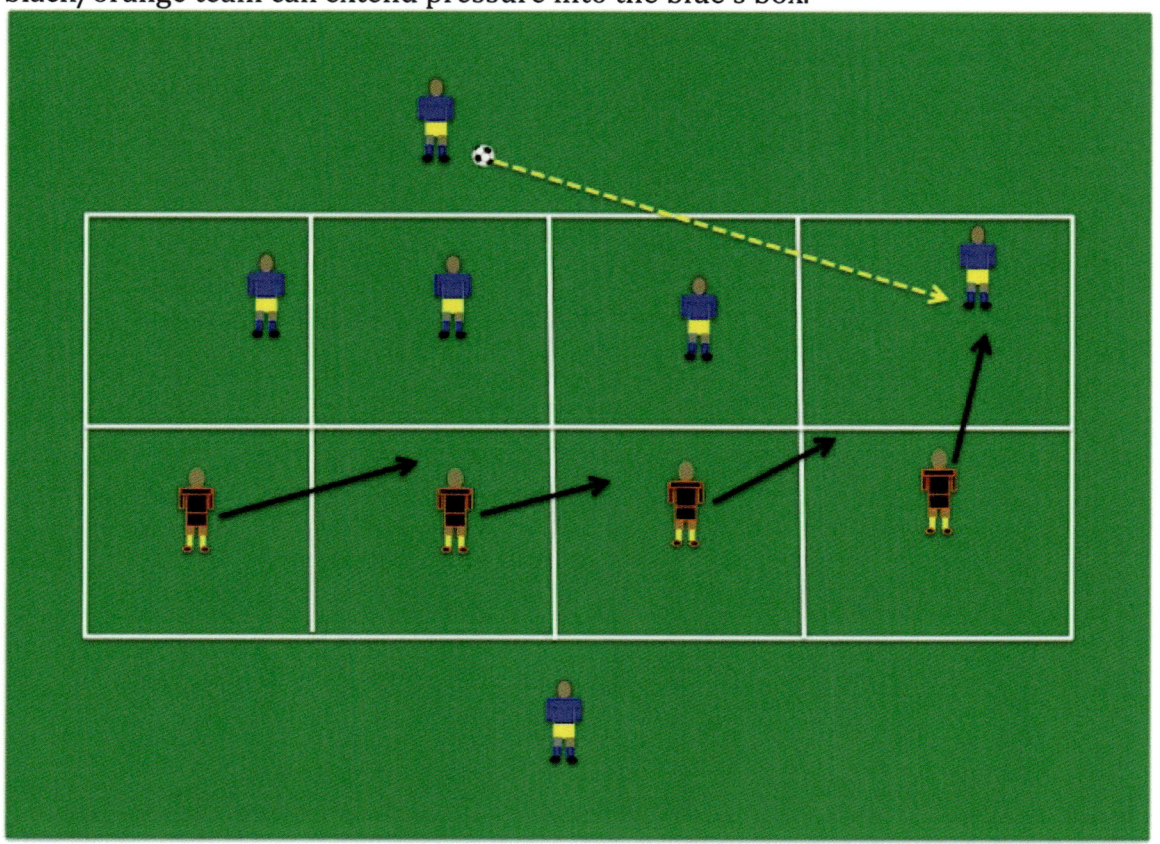

Variation:

The blue team has now added two more outside players making it more difficult for the black/orange team to cover penetrating passes through.

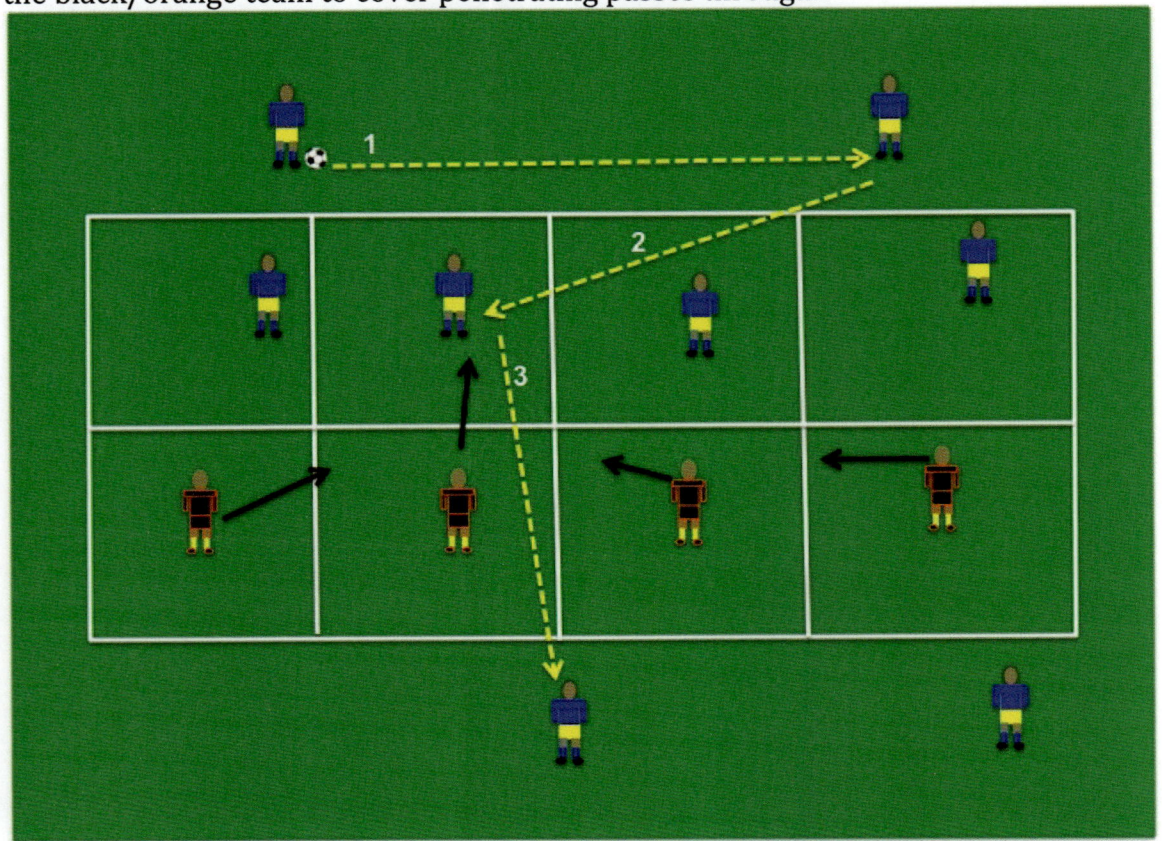

Variation:

Now two new zones are marked off making two 2v1's on the outside of the grid. The black/orange teams single player simulates a forward closing down the ball in front of the midfield four. Play is always 2-touch.

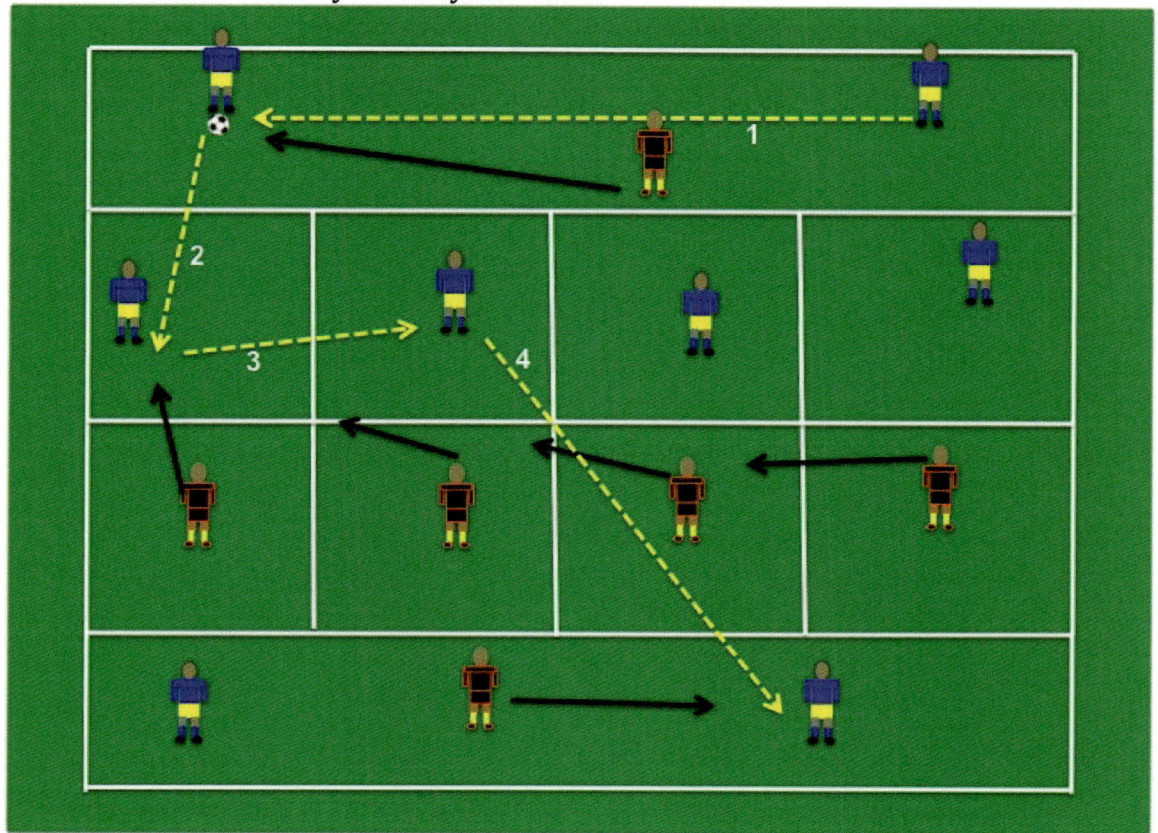

Exercise #2)
The black/orange team have two lines of four players (defensive 4 and midfield 4). The three blue players on the end work the ball back and forth either playing into the two blue in-field players or hit a penetrating ball to the far side group of three blue players. The inside blue players are allowed unlimited touches while outside blue players are 2-touch. The goal of the black/orange team is not to allow penetrating passes by the use of proper positioning and shutting down passing angles.

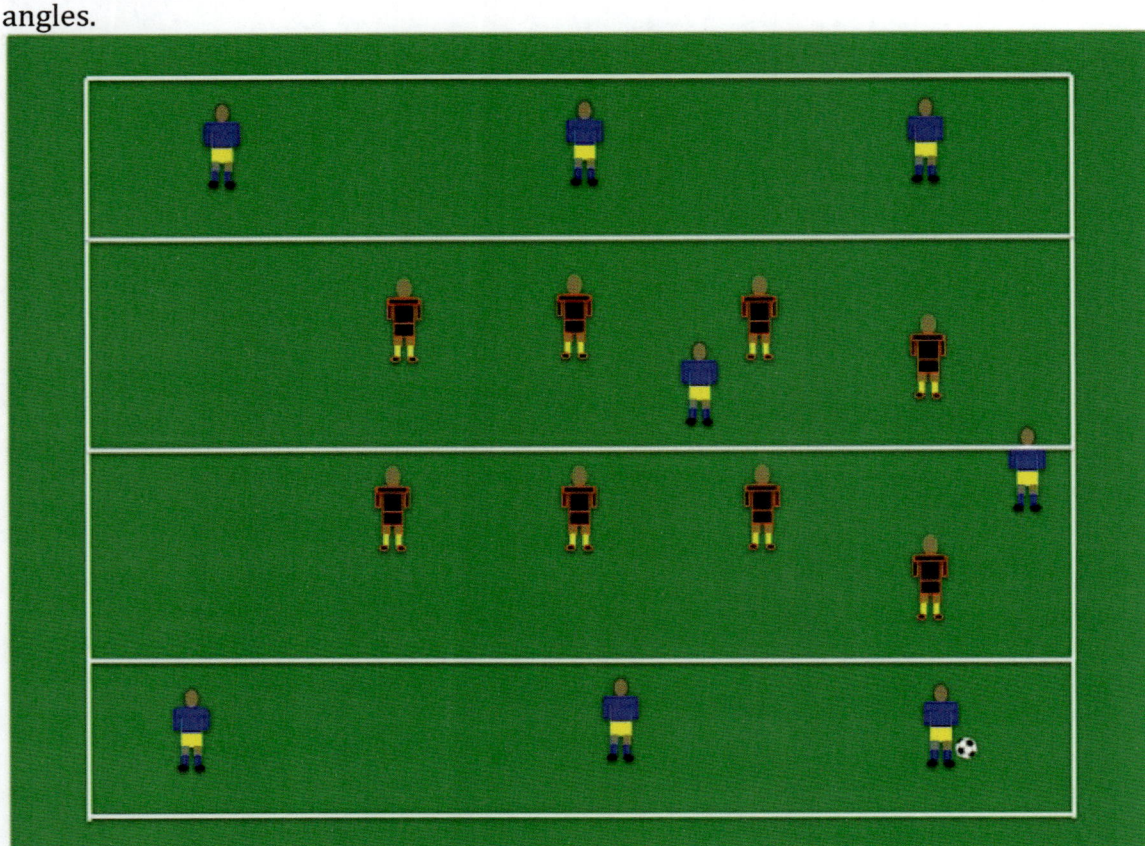

Exercise#3)

When playing the 4-2-3-1 formation – this is a typical pattern practice when pressing play into the sides of the field. The pressing zones are outlined in yellow. Notice the runs of each player and the movement when the ball is switched to the opposite side of the field. The blue team moves the ball from side to side using every player to switch the field. The black/orange team adjusts positions accordingly. This is not a live all out game – rather just a pattern.

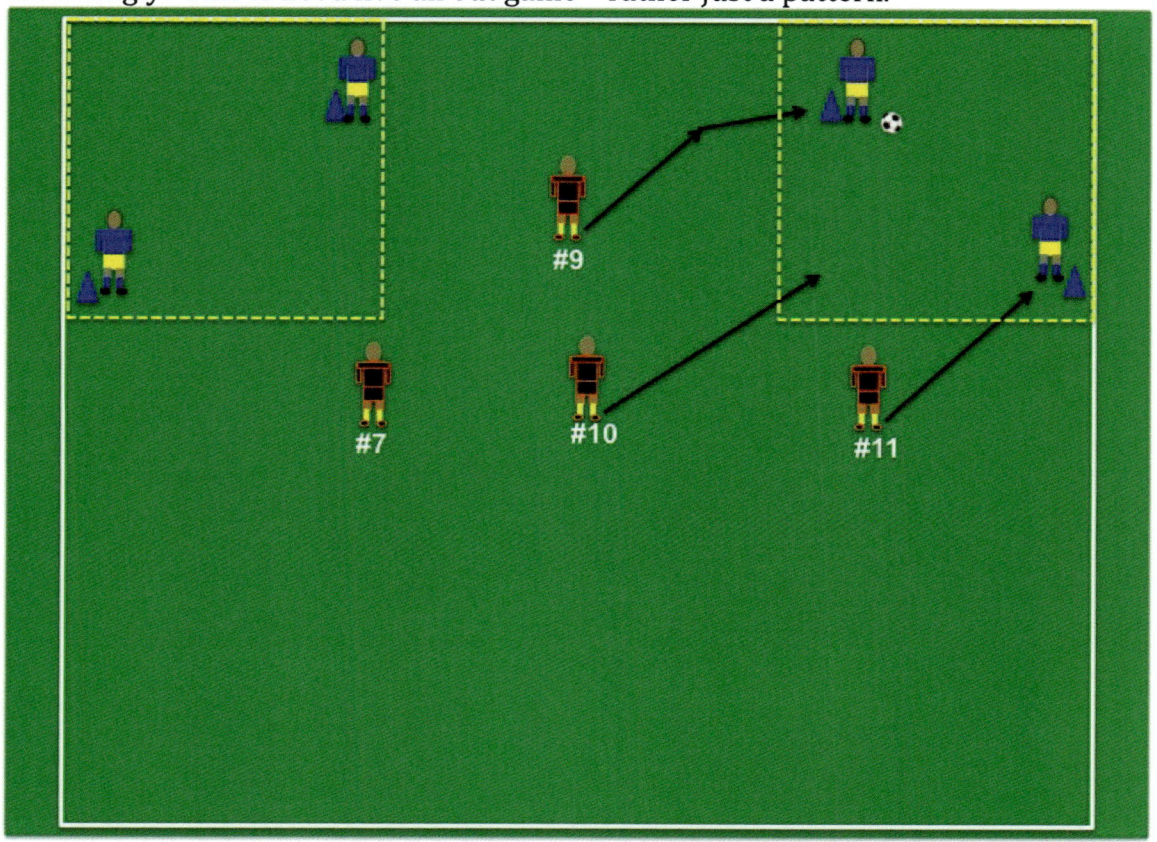

Example of movement when the ball is switched. Notice the movement of the #9 &
#10.

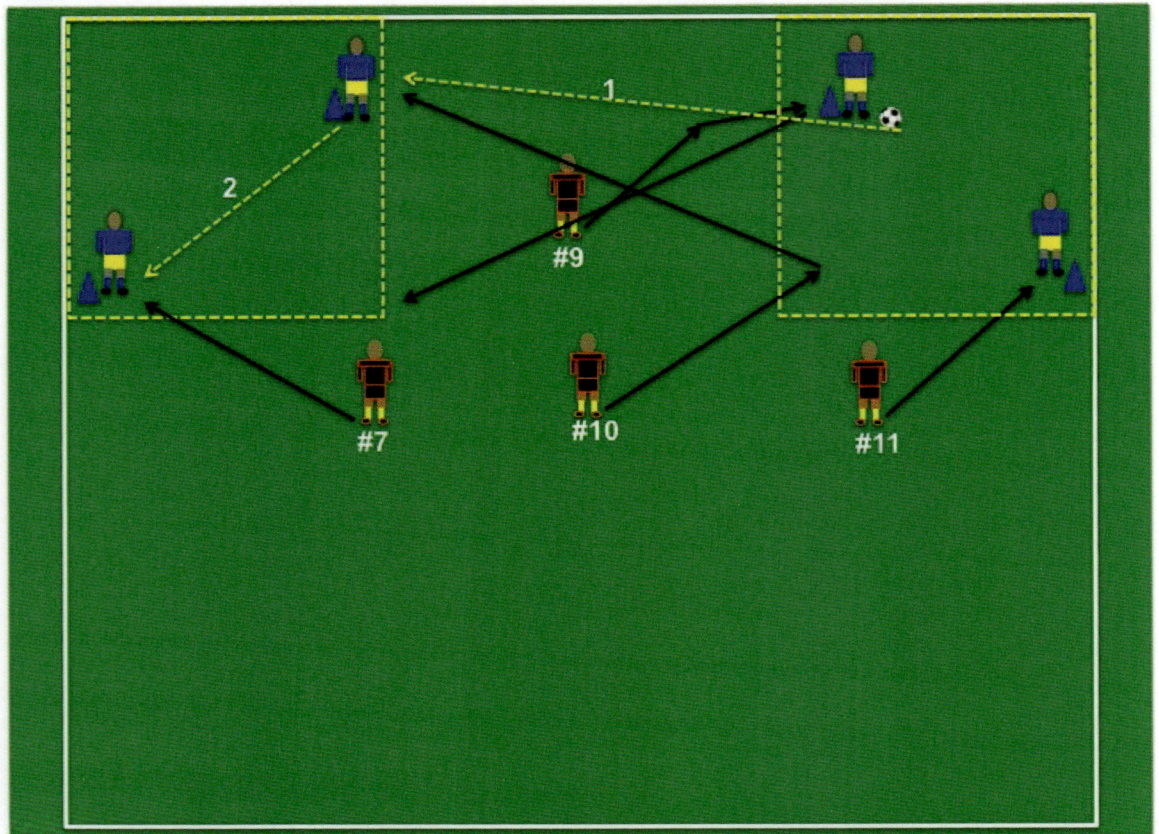

Exercise #4)

This is a live game with 6v4 (plus keeper). The four red defenders are all holding an elastic band that they can't drop. The bands force the group to stay together and move as a coordinated unit. When the blue team wins possession they can drop the bands and play a ball into either blue player that is standing at half field. They have 6 passes or less to get the ball to a blue player at midfield. This is a very creative way to train the back four and their movement!

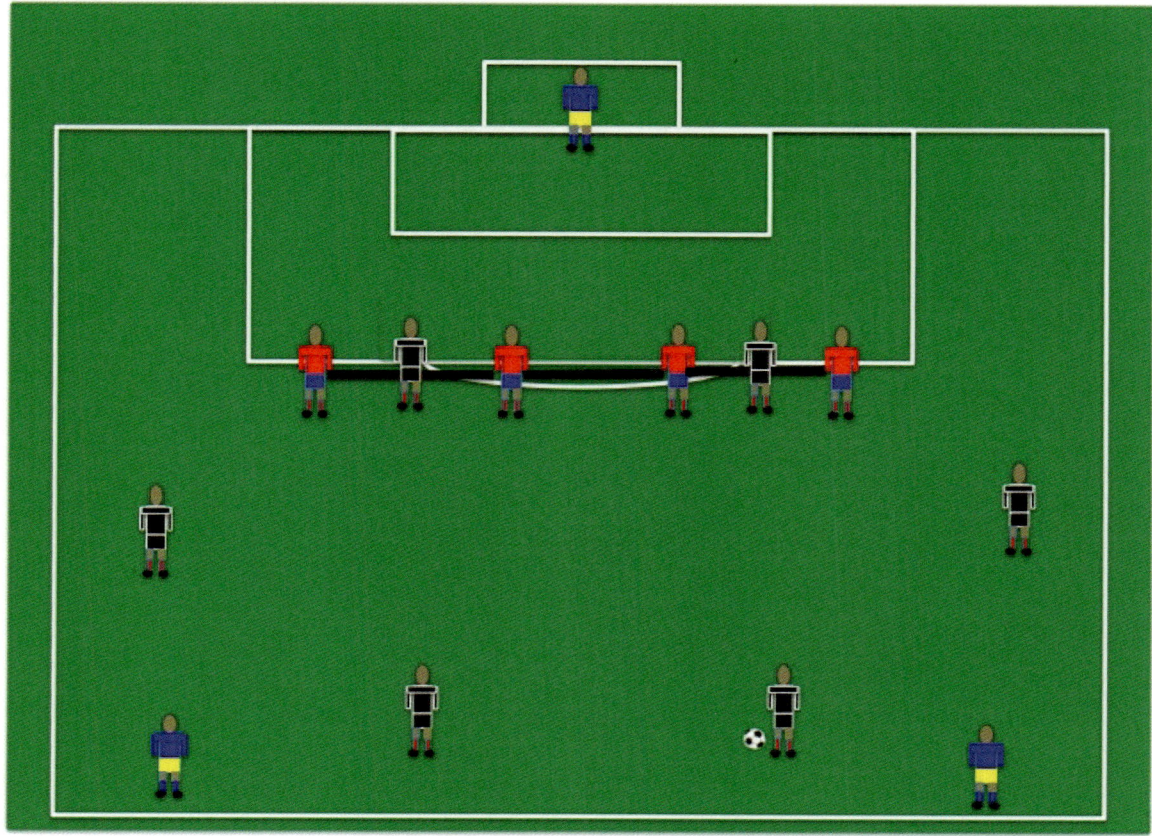

Example #5)
This is the same exercise as #4 but now two red center midfielders are holding one elastic and 2 more players are added on black. The exercise is now 8v6 (plus keeper).

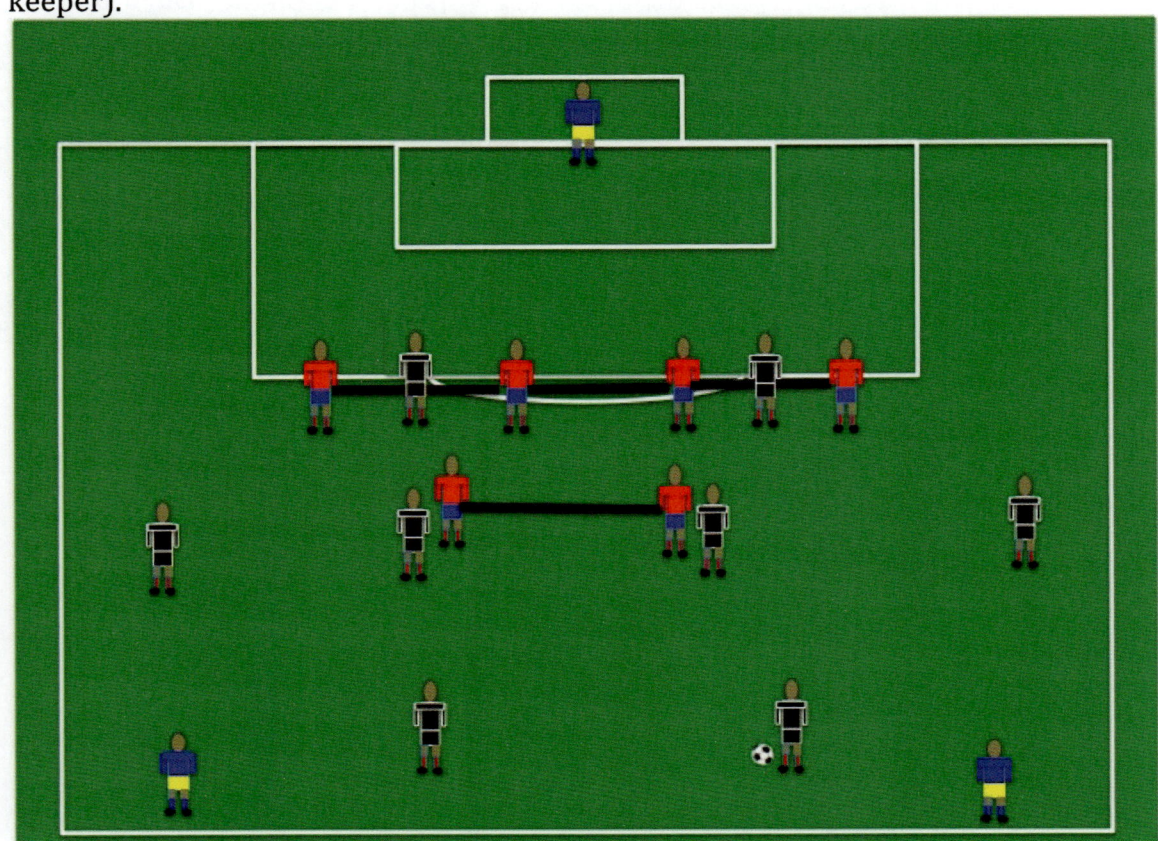

Exercise #7)
Players: 4-12
Grid: 40x20 yards
Instructions & Key Points:
Players sprint fast from the white cone and slow down as they approach the red cone. I like to say "go from tall to small" when closing down a player. It simply means close fast, then slow down, bend your knees and get into a good athletic defending position in front of the attacker. Players will come into the red cone and angle the play with close to a side on stance (making believe the red cone is a real player with the ball). Once the player has closed down the red cones he will shuffle back to the next white cone and continue the same pattern until finished. This simple exercise can be used as a warm-up combined with dynamic movements.

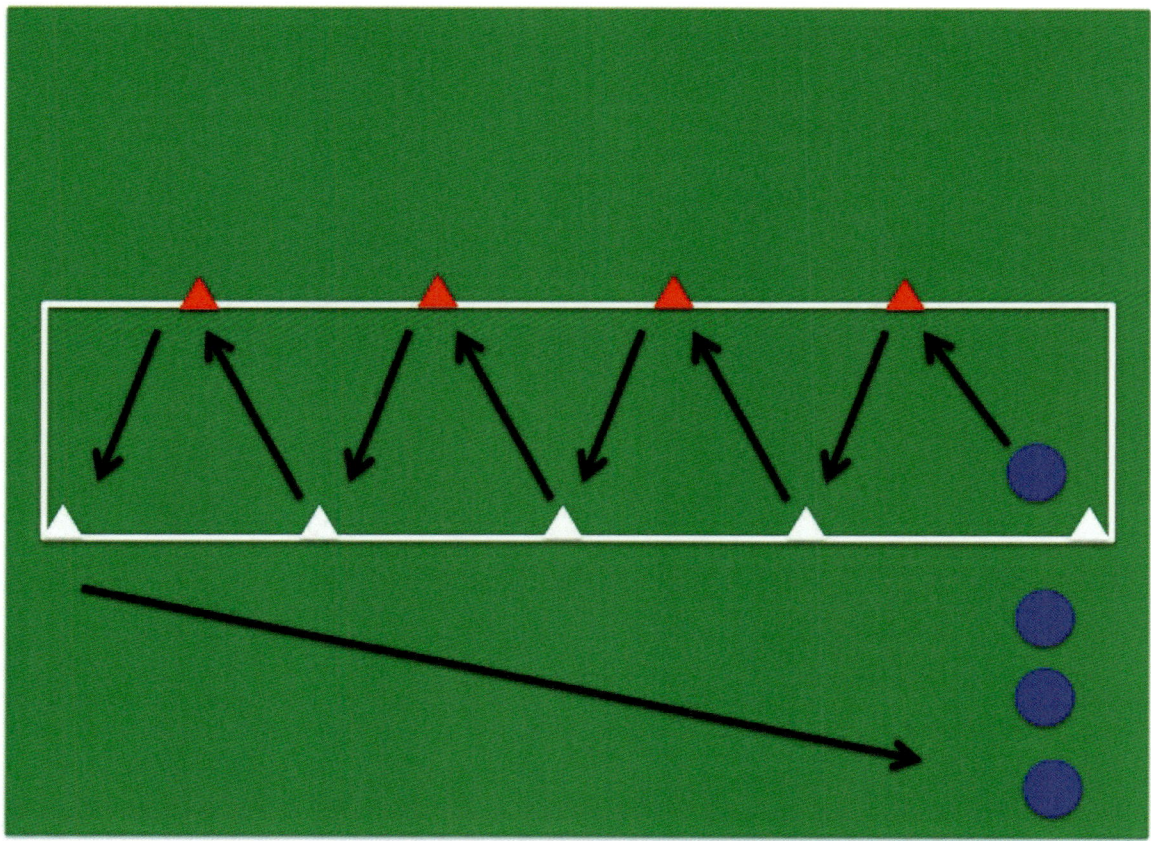

Exercise #8)
Players: 12
Grid: 40x30 yards (divided into 3 separate zones of 40x10 yards each)
Instructions & Key Points:
Three lines of four players each. All lines will be spaced out equal distance apart from each other across the grid. The line in front will pass the ball from one person to the next (slowly at first making sure the back two lines are adjusting to the ball movement). The first defender is pressure, the second defender is cover and the third defender is balance. Both lines should take on the exact same shape as each other. As the two teams adjust quickly the team passing the ball can pass it faster (making the two defensive lines move quicker collectively). Remember to have players call out instructions like "slide right", "slide left", "ball", "back left" and "back right. Make sure players take on the same body shape as the pressuring defender. The players need to close down the ball and have their hips facing the same direction. There should not be any gaps between the players that would allow penetrating passes. The picture below demonstrates the proper player positions in relation to the ball. Notice the pressure, cover and balance.

Ball Position#1.

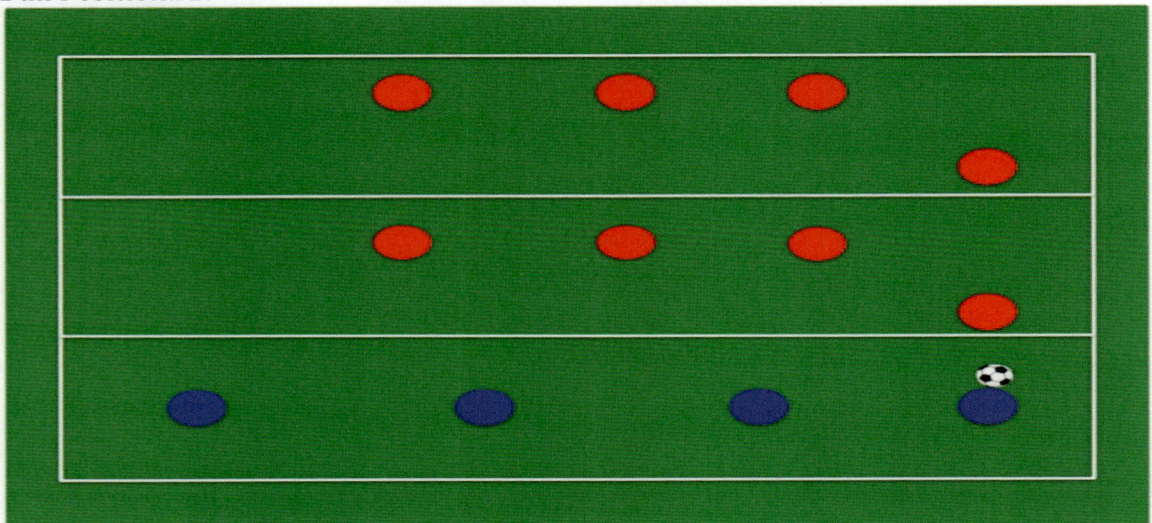

Ball Position#2. Notice the 45 degree angles of support and the pressure, cover and balance.

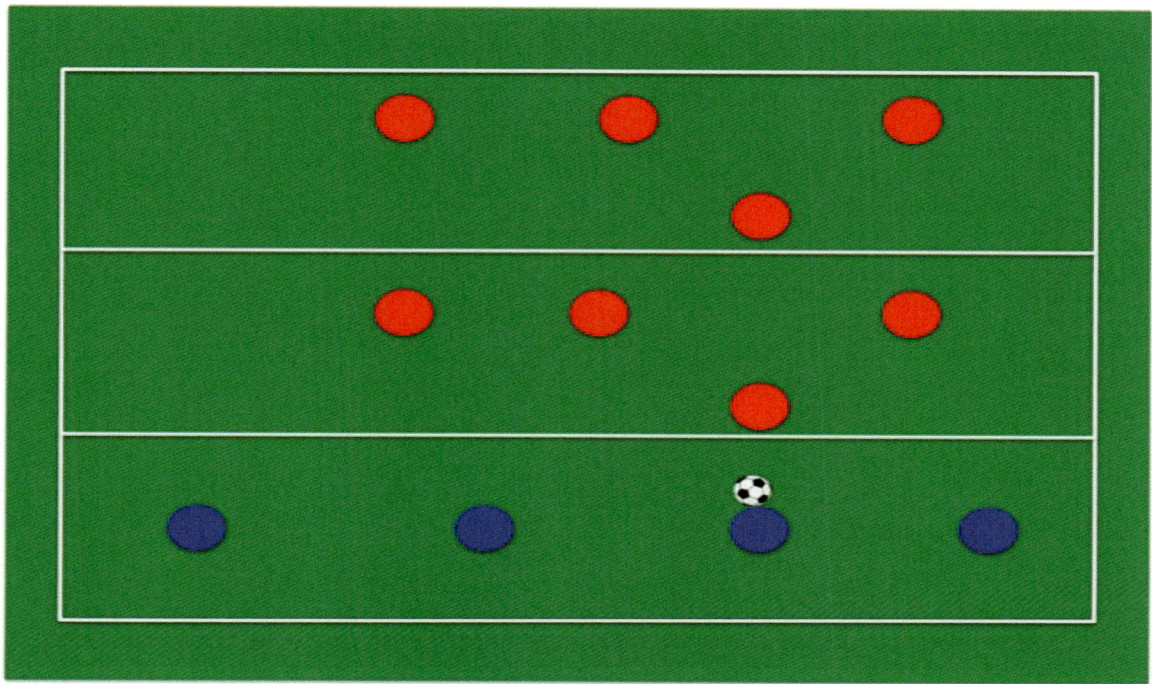

Ball Position#3. Notice the movement involves the entire group.

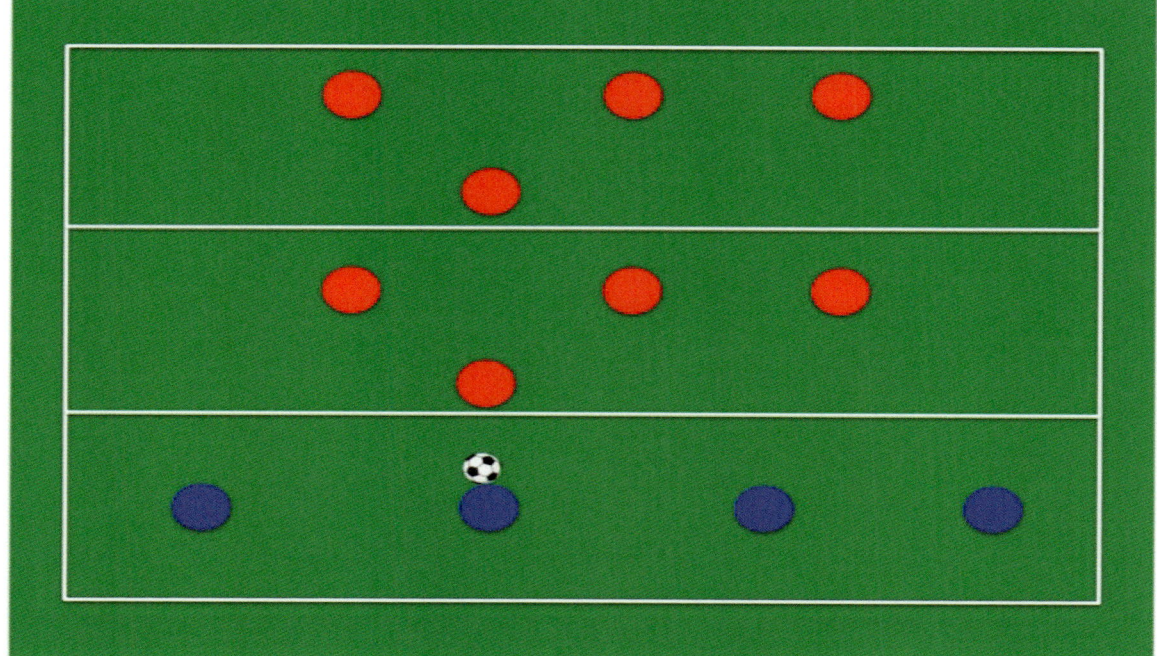

Ball Position #4. The compactness is very good and forward passing angles are shut down.

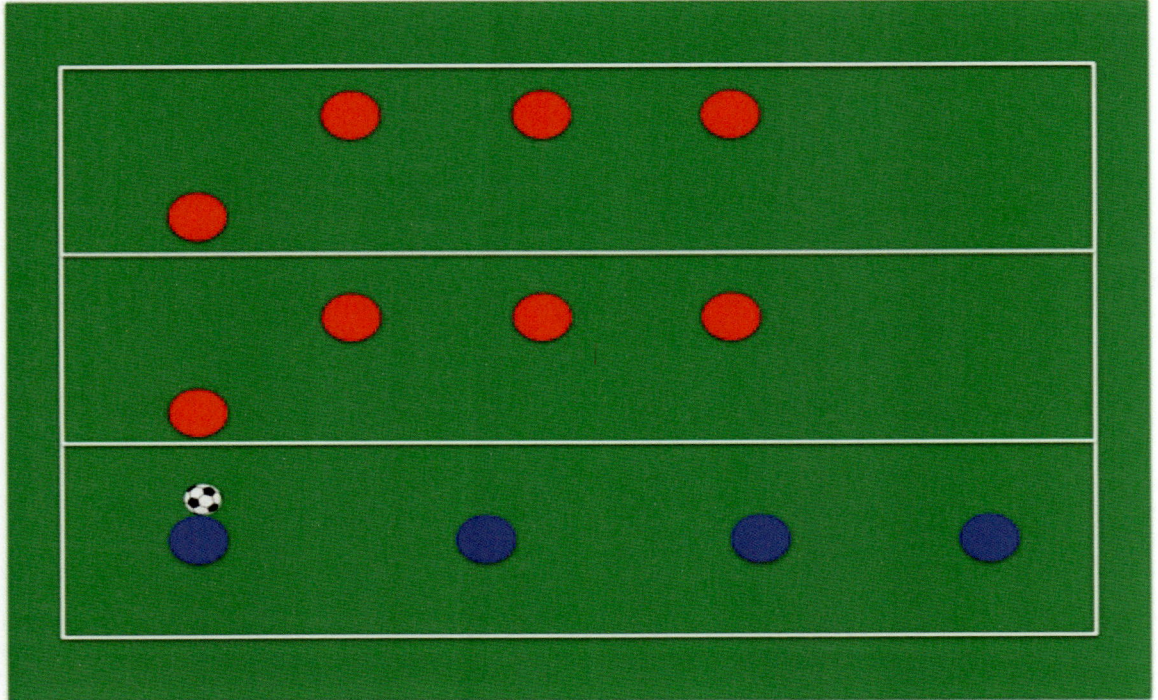

Exercise #9)
Players: 12
Grid: 40x30 yards (divided into 3 separate zones of 40x10 yards each)
Instructions & Key Points:
Three lines of four players each. The two teams in the end zones must try and pass the ball through the middle zone to the team in the far zone. The defending line of four players in the middle will be trying to stop any passes coming through. If the defending team in the middle wins the ball, play starts again with the ball in one of the end zone. Rotate the defending team out every 3 minutes. The unit shape should be identical to drill#2.

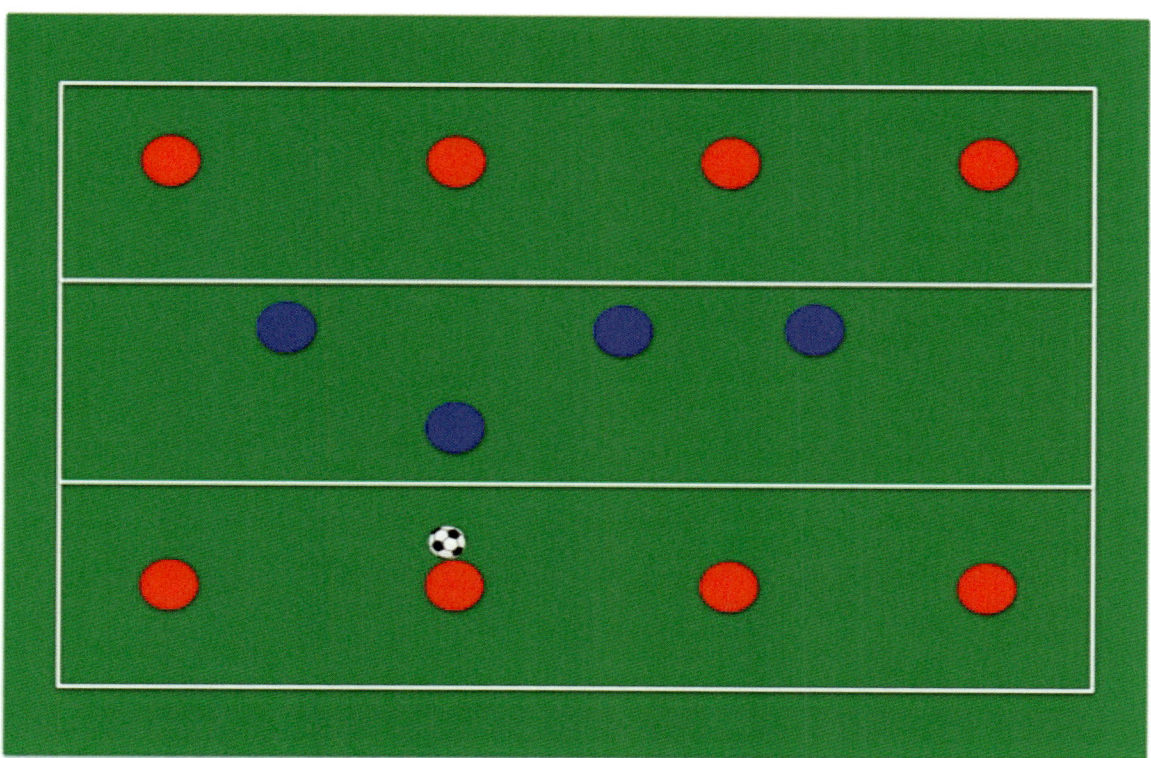

Exercise #10)
Players: 12
Grid: 40x40 yards (divided into 4 separate zones of 40x10 yards each)
Instructions & Key Points:
The red team must try and play through the blue team to the other red team on the ground. If the blue team intercepts the pass they must try and successfully play to the other blue team. The team in possession can pass the ball in their own zone until a through pass presents itself. The entire time the defensive team is adjusting there shape to the position of the ball. Pressure, Cover, balance and compactness as a unit is necessary to be successful in this drill.

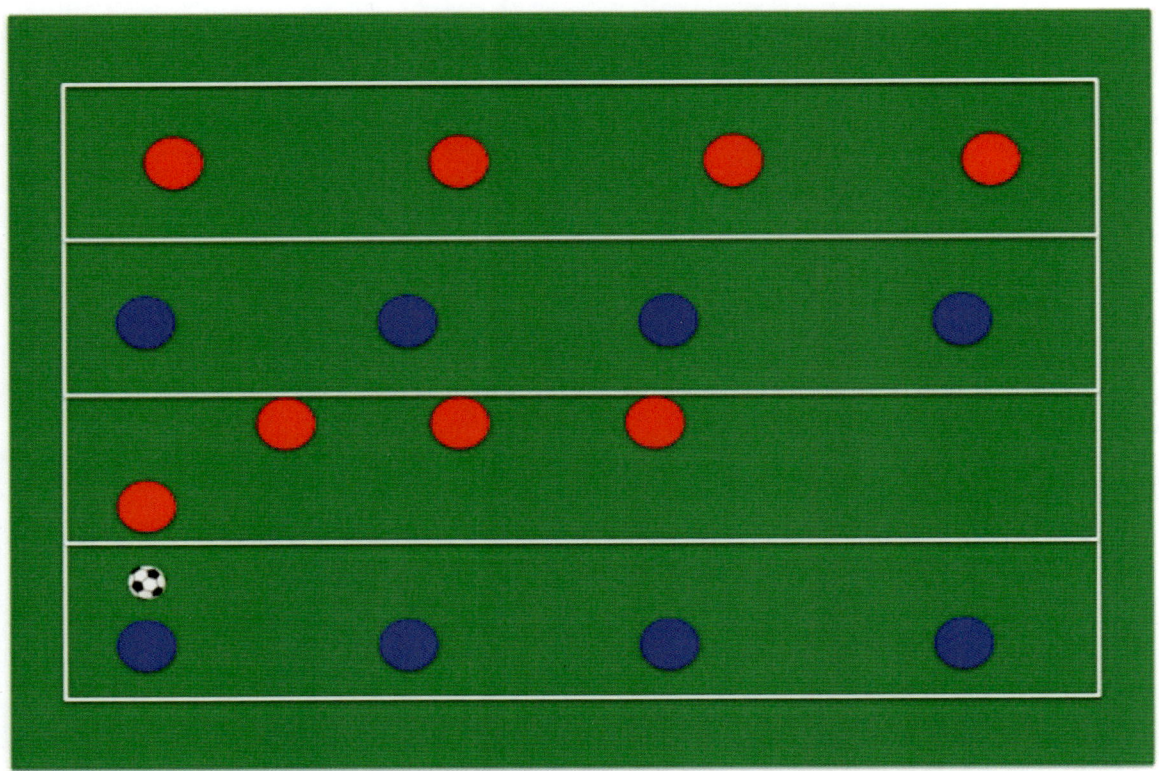

Exercise #11)
Players: 8
Grid: 45x40 yards (line of confrontation 15 yards out from both end lines)
Instructions & Key Points:
The red team must score on the two red cone goals while the blue team must score on the two blue cone goals. The red team uses the red line as their line of confrontation and the blue team uses the blue line as their line of confrontation. Teams are not allowed to pressure past the line of confrontation. This drill focuses on proper line defending using pressure, cover, balance, proper recovery runs and zonal marking (man marking in your zones).   Make sure the line is in the proper position when defending. The attacking team needs to have good movement to make the defending team problem solve and adjust. Offside does apply.

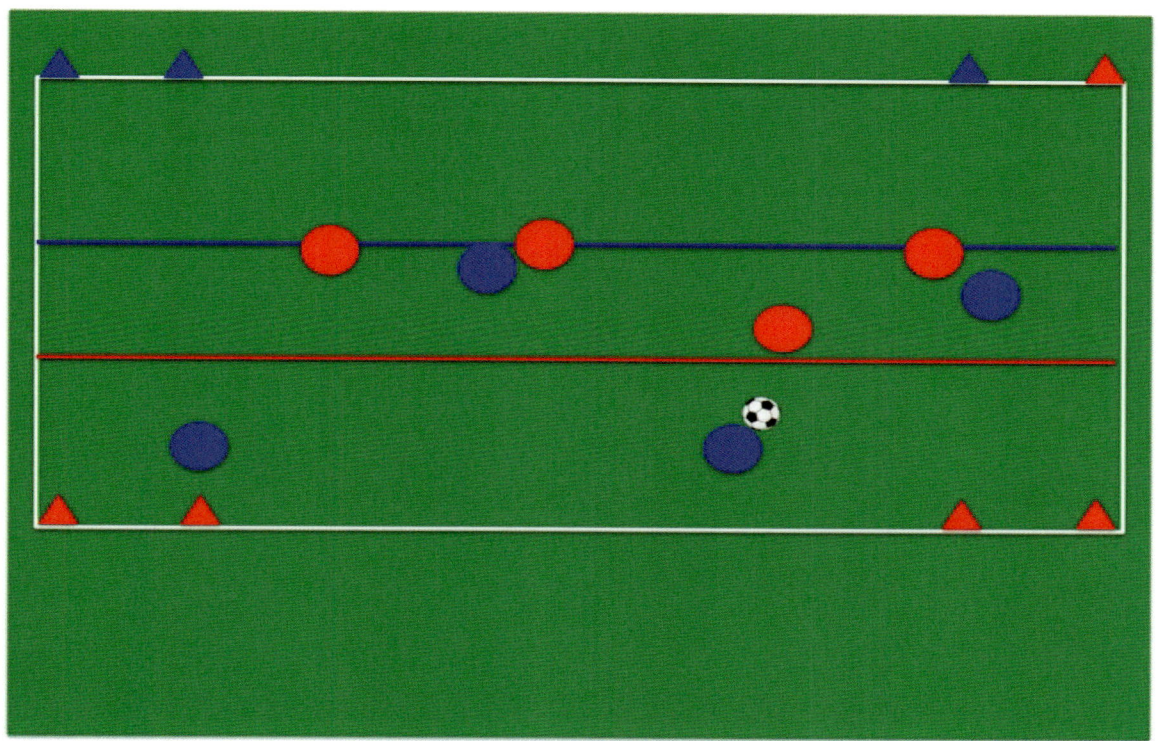

Exercise #12)
Players: 15-21
Grid: Half Field with a grid extending 25 yards out from top of the 18 yard box

Instructions & Key Points:
This drill is 8v6 with only the 2 forwards starting inside the grid. The 6 outside players move the ball clockwise around the grid. The outside players are looking for an opening to play the ball inside to the forward's feet. The 2 defensive midfielders are screening the forwards making it difficult for the ball to be played into the forwards. If the ball is passed around the outside of the grid and ends up with the last player, the game goes live into a half field 8v6 game to goal. If the ball is passed inside to a forward at anytime the game goes live as well. Anytime the blue team intercepts the ball they will try and score on any of the 3 small goals at the half field line.

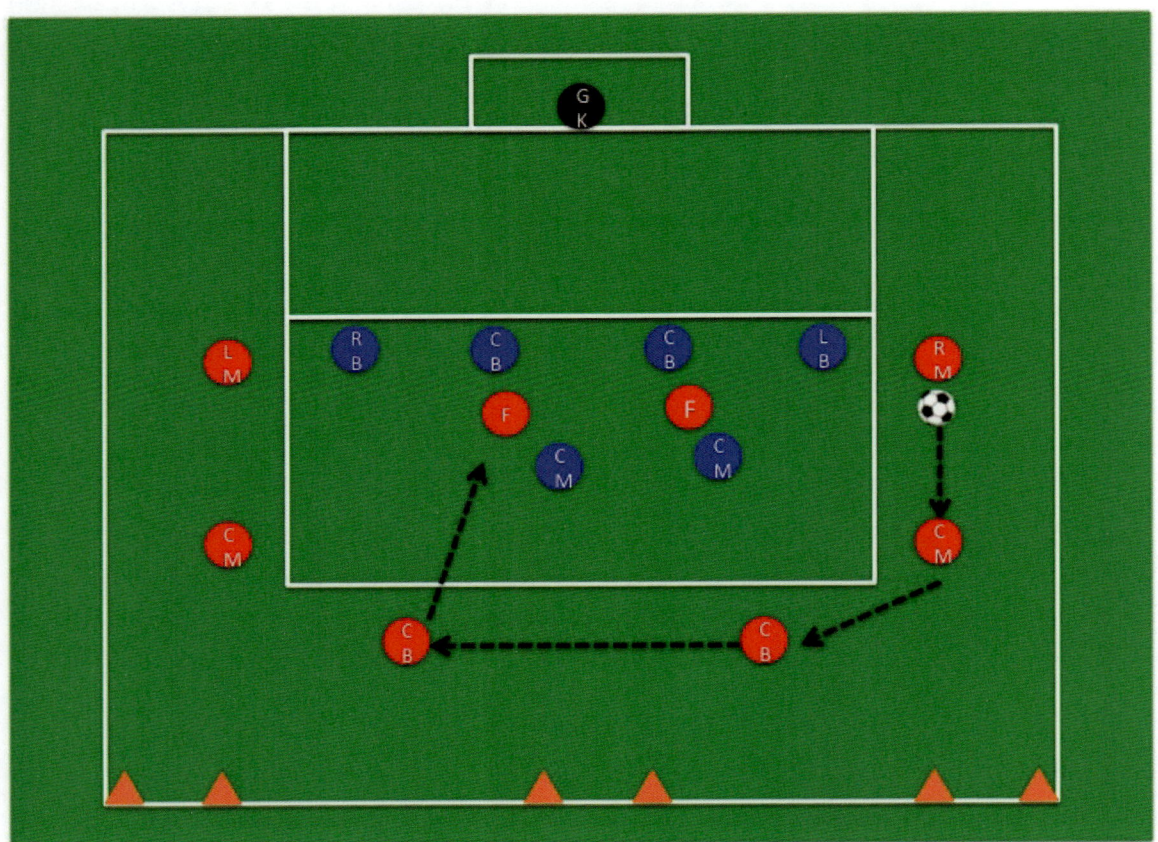

Printed in Great Britain
by Amazon.co.uk, Ltd.,
Marston Gate.